ORACLE PERFORMANCE TUNING EXPERT

100 POWERFUL TIPS

Also by Christopher Lawson

The Art & Science of Oracle Performance Tuning

Snappy Interviews: 100 Questions to Ask Oracle DBAs

ORACLE PERFORMANCE TUNING EXPERT
100 Powerful Tips

Christopher Lawson

author of

**The Art & Science of
Oracle Performance Tuning**

and

**Snappy Interviews: 100 Questions
to Ask Oracle DBAs**

Bassocantor Books
San Francisco

Bassocantor Reviews
P.O. Box 2495
Dublin, California 94568

Printed in the United States of America.

Oracle Performance Tuning Expert: 100 Powerful Tips
Christopher Lawson – 1st ed.

ISBN-10: 1-9860-2919-0
ISBN-13: 9-781-9860-2919-3

www.Bassocantor.com

Printed in the United States of America
First Edition
10 9 8 7 6 5 4 3 2 1

Table of Contents

INTRODUCTION

Performance Tuning is the best job in the world. Well, okay, there might be a few other jobs that are better—but it's still a fascinating, rewarding job.

Over the course of twenty years, I have solved over 10,000 performance problems. After a few thousand, I began to realize, "Hey, there seems to be a pattern here!" After a while, one sees a pattern in the process, and begins to understand what ideas work, and which do not.

In this book, I list my top 100 performance tips. These are tips and lessons that I use myself every day. Some of the tips were originally suggested in *The Art & Science of Oracle Performance Tuning,* and some were mentioned in *Snappy Interviews.*

Here's an astonishing observation:

> *The essence of the performance tuning process has stayed the same over 20 years.*

Naturally, there are new or difference features in the database, but the performance analyst pretty much does the same thing. Twenty years ago, the DBA still asked the user, "What seems to be the problem?"

I hope you find this book useful in all your performance tuning tasks. I often post new ideas or articles on my blog, *Bassocantor.com.* You can also comment on my articles, or submit questions at this site.

Christopher Lawson
Dublin, California
April 15, 2018

HOW TO APPROACH PERFORMANCE TUNING

A big part of performance tuning is how you approach the problem. If you get off to a wrong start, you are doomed. If you get nothing else right, be sure to get the approach right!

"I Like to Guess at Root Cause."

The true way to become a performance-tuning expert is not through clever technical sophistication, but rather a good understanding of the *overall approach*. Many extremely bright engineers do poorly at performance tuning because of a faulty approach.

To be effective, the performance expert must have a flexible approach that can address the different requirements of each performance assignment. In other words, the DBA must wear different "hats" as the performance tuning process enfolds. The effective performance analyst realizes that the methods used must *adapt* to the particular problem and to the people involved.

START #1 USE THE "PHYSICIAN-TO-MAGICIAN" APPROACH

There is no single "performance-fixing machine," by which a solution magically emerges as the DBA "cranks the handle." Each problem requires fact-gathering and analysis. An adaptable approach, not a "silver bullet" is the key.

The performance DBA must use *different methods* at *different phases* of the process. This is one reason why a "silver bullet" approach, or the magical "tool" method is rarely an adequate answer.

Here is a summary of the "Physician-to-Magician" process:

- **The Oracle Doctor:** The kindly doctor listens to his patients. He asks, "What is the problem?" and then follows up to get the details.

- **The Oracle Detective:** Here, the Oracle analyst dons the hat of the detective. The main objective in this step is to *recreate and quantify* the problem

- **The Oracle Pathologist:** The analyst tries to find the root cause of the problem and isolates the "disease" that is causing our database-patient the distress.

- **The Oracle Artist:** The analyst switches to creative mode as he tries to synthesize a solution that is technically correct, as well as acceptable to the organization.

- **The Oracle Magician:** Finally, the Oracle Magician implements the solution and reports the improvement to management.

When any of us visit a doctor, the doctor will soon ask, "What seems to be the trouble?" In medical clinics, this is called finding the "chief complaint." The DBA doctor must do the same thing. For instance, he may ask the question, "How long is the query delay?" or "When does the problem occur?"

After defining the problem, the next step is investigation. Here, the DBA changes hats from physician to detective. The main objective in this step is to *recreate and quantify* the problem. The DBA-detective will strive to find the actual elapsed time of the query, or the number of disk and logical reads that are performed. In many cases, the DBA-detective will discover that the problem has nothing to do with the database at all. Sometimes, he will conclude that there isn't even a problem!

After the detective has gathered clues (and confirmed that a problem really exists), the Oracle Pathologist tries to find the root cause of the problem and isolate the "disease" that is causing our database-patient so much distress. At this point, we have a great deal of good information, so there will be no need to make guesses. The Oracle physician and Oracle detective have given us "their files," which contain a great amount of useful information. This information will help guide us to the source of the problem.

With the root cause of the problem identified, the task of the *Oracle Artist* is to create an acceptable solution. Whereas previous stages have required analysis, this stage requires *synthesis*. The Oracle Artist will have to consider the particular environment in fashioning a solution that is not just technically accurate, but also feasible. Both technical and organizational issues will need to be considered, so that the final solution is both technical accurate and *acceptable* to the customer.

Finally, the Oracle Magician will implement and confirm the solution devised by the previous steps. This is the most exciting part of the whole process; we now *activate* a solution that has been carefully prepared to resolve the performance bottleneck. As a final step, we will also *quantify* the performance improvement for a subsequent report to management.

With the completion of step 5, our database "patient," formerly so sick and sluggish, now skips out of the "infirmary," with a clean bill of health. His "chart" has been updated to show his new vital signs, with a copy to grateful "hospital management."

Understanding, Not Trickery

Ironic as it sounds, the successful performance expert will strive to *avoid* tricks. That is, the seasoned DBA or designer knows that special setups or tricky code should be *avoided*. While, the results achieved by a competent Oracle analyst might *resemble* trickery, the process is really based on good understanding of database operation.

In fact, using exotic solutions, understandable only by the select few in the "DBA-guru club," is a cruel disservice to your employer. The reason for this is simple. In future years, the firm will probably not understand what you did (or *why*). Documentation that you may have left will probably be lost. Other DBAs who were familiar with your work will be gone. The result of the tricky solution by the tricky DBA is that the application is almost impossible to maintain.

START #2 ROOT CAUSE FIRST, SOLUTION SECOND

This is so obvious that one might wonder why I even mention it. But this logical error is pervasive. It is most common with bright young engineers with limited experience.

Jumping to a solution is easy, fun, and takes no competence in the subject matter; anybody can do it! Truly finding the root cause, however, takes labor, time and competence. That's no fun!

I often get requests to solve a performance issue where the requester already assumes some type of solution. For example, he or she might say, "Please check indexes on Table X," or "Please make sure we have good stats on Table Y." At other times, the in-house customer has already decided that more CPU is needed, since the processors are maxed out all the time.

Typically, I don't give much credence to suggestions like these, because they are really just *guesses* at the root cause. Maybe they're right, but probably not. In these cases, my approach is to say something like, "How about I go find the root cause first?" When stated this way, almost everyone sees the logic in this approach.

One of my former managers at work puts it this way: "Don't try to 'solutionize' before you know the root cause." Nicely stated!

START #3 FOCUS ON THE *CUSTOMER'S* PROBLEM

In order to maximize value for our employer, we must then strive to fix *their* problems. This directed focus is important whether we are analyzing a tough performance problem, or simply setting up backups. The entire process must have its end goal service to the customer.

The Physician-to-Magician approach recognizes this focus on meeting the needs of the customer. The problem statement is always from the perspective of the *customer*, not the DBA. That is why we put such a great emphasis on listening in stage 1. Without patient listening, the performance analyst may not solve what is truly important to the customer. That would mean falling once more into the old trap, "Solving the wrong problem."

Of course, the customer may be completely in error in suggesting that the database is at fault. The user may simply be mistaken. That is why the part of the process is gathering facts to confirm and quantify the problem. These additional facts will help the tuning specialist see how the customer's perspective relates to what is happening in the database. What the customer sees on the "outside" is often surprisingly different from what the DBA sees on the "inside."

This customer focus continues throughout the tuning process. For instance, the Oracle "Artist" must fashion a solution that is acceptable to the designers and others in the firm. Some problems may have many solutions—but not all will be acceptable or appropriate. Even in the final stage, where the Oracle Magician is the main player, the DBA "closes the loop" by documenting how his solution solves the client's original problem. This confirms that the implemented solution has actually met the needs of the customer.

START #4 ADMIT YOU COULD BE WRONG

In order to maintain a positive atmosphere, it is important to make it clear that the DBA is not immune from making blunders. In fact, it is very possible that the DBA could make even *more* errors, with *bigger consequences* than others do!

It hurts to even admit the possibility, but we must face the facts: DBAs do occasionally make errors. In fact, sometimes we make *big* errors. When this happens, the wisest course of action is to readily admit our blunder; let the users "have their day."

Working on a team where first and foremost, everyone is working to solve a *problem* takes away any concern about blame for a mistake. In most cases, most competent software professionals are "big enough" to accept responsibility without becoming defensive. The consequences of this attitude are that the team has a *huge advantage* over their competitors.

A frank admission that one could be wrong has an immediate effect on the team. It tells everyone that the individual is a "team player," not out for personal glory at the expense of others. It goes a long way to establishing a relationship of trust with co-workers.

When there has been a clear mistake, admitting the error also diffuses the entire issue. After all, once someone has admitted that they made a mistake, what more can be said? After a "Mea Culpa," there is nothing more to say. The point has been made, and everyone wishes to "just go on."

START #5 DO NOT ASSUME USER ACCURATELY REPORTS PROBLEM

First of all, the Oracle Detective must actually verify, or *confirm* the performance problem. Just as a police detective immediately "looks for the body," the Oracle Detective must be absolutely sure that any database-related problem really exists.

Here's the key point: The facts that are reported to the DBA are oftentimes completely in error. That is, the purported performance bottleneck *simply does not exist!* This can happen, for instance, if the user is misled by some oddity in the application that resembles a performance problem. At other times, there might be a problem, but one that is completely different than what the user believes.

Therefore, so that no one wastes any more time, it is necessary to first confirm that a problem even exists. Fortunately, there are many ways to accomplish this confirmation

Ways To Verify A Problem

Each site will be a little different, but there are several methods that can be used at most locations. The exact method chosen is really a matter of personal preference; no one method is mandatory.

In order to confirm a performance problem, the Oracle Detective can usually perform any of these steps:

- ✓ Re-run the application in a controlled environment
- ✓ Check the application run logs
- ✓ Query the V$Sql view to find the SQL statements
- ✓ Monitor the application using a tool.

Re-run the application in a controlled environment

One very simple way to verify a problem is to re-run the application, using the same parameters as noted in the original problem statement. Sometimes this can be done on the production system without interfering with other users. At other times, this option is not possible, because the application might change some critical data, or otherwise interfere with other production users.

In some cases, it is best to watch the end-user as he executes the program. This is valuable, as it is always helpful for the DBA to understand more about the application. A side benefit of watching the user demonstrate the problem is that your customer will understand that you are *serious* about solving their problem. They will appreciate your interest. It tells them that you do "make house calls."

Another advantage in watching the user re-stage the problem is that hints about the problem are frequently revealed. For instance, upon seeing an odd error message, the user might say something like, "Oh, we always get that problem. You can ignore that." Of course, the user could be *wrong*—perhaps the funny error message is critical to solving the problem.

Check the Application Logs

Another easy way to verify a performance problem is to find out what kind of logs the application writes, and then review each of the logs for significant delays. Once again, this is a simple step, but easily (and often) overlooked.

Many applications, especially those involving large batch jobs, keep track of long-running processes. Sometimes, the application designer has been clever enough to record the start and stop times for key steps in an application. These type of run logs make the job of the Oracle Detective much easier.

More Sophisticated Techniques

There are also some more sophisticated techniques for gathering clues and quantifying the performance degradation. These methods require a little more work, but are often well worth the effort. Perhaps my favorite method is *wait-event analysis,* using the ASH tables. We provide several hints specifically explaining ways to use the ASH tables.

START #6 CONSIDER *OTHER* SYSTEMS THAT CAUSE BOTTLENECKS

Performance problems do not confine themselves to just one subsystem. For instance, there will always be at least *some* sort of application that access the Oracle database over *some* sort of network. Clearly, Oracle databases cannot achieve anything by themselves; useful programs must be designed to retrieve and format the data in a manner helpful to the users.

To start, there are *three* subsystems that will likely be involved in every performance problem: *Database, application,* and *network*. In addition, there are oftentimes other subsystems involved, such as web servers, application servers, report servers, remote databases and data feeds, etc. Theoretically, even the client setup can impact performance.

Amazingly, many beginner (and even senior) analysts spend *days* troubleshooting a performance problem without even bothering to identify which subsystem could conceivably be responsible! Many hours are wasted chasing performance issues on systems that are completely uninvolved!

Identify The *Real* Contributors

Since there will always be multiple subsystems that could *theoretically* be the cause of a performance problem, it will be necessary to determine which subsystems are contributing in *reality* to the performance problem that is being analyzed.

Of course, each subsystem will likely add *some* delay; which is normal. Even a perfectly operating network with massive bandwidth will induce a fraction of a second delay. Normally, of course, such small delays can be safely ignored. (Of course, if the performance problem really were a sub-second issue, even these miniscule delays would have to be considered.)

Putting aside these trivial performance delays, the analyst should look for large, unexpected delays in each candidate subsystem that are roughly the same size as the performance problem. Thus, if the users are complaining of a 10-minute delay, don't waste your time trying to tune SQL code that contributes a total of 10 *seconds* delay. The 10-second delay might become important later on, but is probably not relevant now.

START #7 FIND A ROOT CAUSE BY *SIMPLIFYING*

I have used this technique countless times. This approach is especially useful when applied to SQL tuning, but the concept can be applied to many technical issues. When applied to SQL code, the idea is to remove irrelevant distractions, such as formatting, irrelevant functions, simple lookup tables, etc. from the query.

Oftentimes, what begins like a very formidable problem looks less intimidating once these distractions are removed. This simple step helps everything look much simpler, and helps the analyst focus on the real "core" of the performance problem.

Simplifying SQL queries

SQL queries will often contain a huge numbers of fields in the "Select" list. To further complicate the issue, a variety of different functions may also be used—functions such as TRIM, UPPER, TO_CHAR, etc.

The large number of fields and functions often make the task look harder than it really is. If nothing else, a huge *Select* list makes it difficult to see the entire SQL statement on one page, forcing the analyst to shift his attention from page to page. It is amazing how much easier a problem seems when the essential problem can be cleanly listed on a single page.

Reduce a Complicated SQL Query to its *Essence*

The object in simplifying is to reduce the SQL code down to the *essence* of the query (or transaction). This is really half the battle! When the core code can be clearly identified, the analyst has already gone a long way towards finding the root cause.

Once a satisfactory correction has been formulated based on the *simplified* code, the analyst can confirm the solution by repeating the test with the *original* SQL.

Remove Irrelevant Information

A good first step in simplifying is to note which parts of a complicated SQL query have little to do with the performance of the entire SQL statement. For example, certain columns in the *Select* list may be duplicated in other parts of the Select list.

Consider the simple query below. In this case, it looks like the application required that the column Last_Name be listed in two places:

```
Select Last_Name LASTNAME,  Last_Name ||
First_Name FULLNAME
From Emp
Where Emp_No > 1000;
```

In the above query, let's look at the work that the Oracle engine has to perform. Does the Oracle engine retrieve each row twice, since the SQL query specifies the *Last_Name* column twice? No, it does not. The optimizer simply uses the value that was retrieved the first time. In other words, the duplicate columns are redundant, and do not materially affect the optimizer.

This observation is good news for the performance analyst, since many SQL queries contain duplicate fields. The simplification step is clear: For purposes of performance tuning, the original query can be rewritten as:

```
Select Last_Name, First_Name
From Emp
Where Emp_No > 1000;
```

Note that the column titles, *LASTNAME* and *FULLNAME* have also been removed. The application needed these column titles, but we do not. This is another simple step to make things a bit easier (and shorter). The optimizer does not alter its operation just because the output is going to be given a special name. Why not get rid of these distractions?

Remove Irrelevant Functions

Functions that are placed in the *Select* clause are also an unwelcome distraction. Consider the following SQL:

```
Select decode (Acctg_Number, 1, 3), Acctg_Dept
|| '-001'
From Acctg
Where User_id > 100;
```

In this example, the two functions (*decode* and *concatenate*) are simply distractions that complicate our work. The decode function simply substitutes one value for another, and the concatenate operator '||' just appends a few characters. Clearly, neither have any relevance to the execution plan for the SQL statement. The Oracle optimizer will normally not be affected by functions in the Select clause.

The revised SQL code is:

```
Select Acctg_Number, Acctg_Dept
From Acctg
Where User_id > 100;
```

An observer might wonder, "Don't these functions cause the CPU to perform more work?" Yes, they do. The database engine must calculate each function for each row retrieved. If many thousands or millions of rows were being retrieved, this fact would certainly have to be considered. Practically speaking, however, these minor delays will normally be far less than the "real" performance bottleneck. As always, the performance analyst is looking for contributed delays that are "in the ballpark" of the total system delay.

Of course, the presence of one or two functions in the Select clause does not complicate matters too much. Why bother? For one thing, the ability to find the *essential SQL* is a useful habit to encourage. Get in the habit of "zooming in" on the core issue while discarding the "noise."

The habit of simplifying SQL will prove most valuable when "monster" SQL queries need to be analyzed. What seemed like a trivial change in a short SQL statement could become a substantial simplification when faced with a SQL statement that joins a dozen tables.

Simplify—but not too Far!

The trick in the simplification approach is to make the original SQL simpler—without changing the *essence* of the code. That is, the revised SQL should require the Oracle engine to accomplish the same work as the original SQL. Thus, if the original SQL requires the optimizer to join certain tables, then obviously, the simplified SQL must retain this condition. Otherwise, the subsequent analysis will not be helpful, and the proposed solution will fail when tried with the original SQL.

START #8 CHECK SIMPLE THINGS FIRST

I confess, I have been fooled more than once by forgetting to check the most simple things. Some basic steps, which only require a few minutes to perform, include:

- ✓ Check the alert log for the database being queried. Note any unusual error messages, such as space or rollback problems.
- ✓ Check for any indications of space problems.
- ✓ Confirm that a file "auto-extend" has not met its limit.
- ✓ Verify that the archive log file system is not full.
- ✓ Verify that the maximum number of users has not been hit.
- ✓ Verify that the file system holding the listener.log is not full.
- ✓ Verify that statistics have been generated.

For any particular site experiencing trouble, there will likely be other pertinent logs to check. For instance, web-based applications will certainly have logs related to the web-server. Checking these logs first can save the analyst a lot of trouble later.

Error Messages

It is also important to ask the users if they have experienced any error messages, such as "ORA-nnn" errors. Unfortunately, applications frequently return misleading error messages, but occasionally the application error message is useful.

Note that users often forget about an error message, or believe that it is unimportant! Do not assume that the users have given you all the information available.

Remember that a great many performance problems are *trivial* to correct! It is frequently not necessary to perform sophisticated analyses, as some problems are oftentimes extremely simple to correct. Believe it or not, many performance issues still arise because of wrong stats. On countless occasions, I have found that the stats shows 0 rows for a table, which actually had millions of rows.

START #9 *LAST* CAUSE IS NOT THE SAME AS *ROOT* CAUSE

When faced with a new problem to troubleshoot, many smart people immediate ask the question, "What Changed?" This seems logical, but is usually not the best way to approach a performance problem.

By looking for recent changes, you are assuming that everything was indeed fine until the problem was reported. That is a bad assumption-- especially in the world of performance tuning. Just because something was running pretty well before, that doesn't mean it was well-designed; it could just mean you "got away" with a poor design.

In philosophy, the most recent cause is called the "Proximate" cause. The root cause is called the "Ultimate" cause. Two examples will clarify:

Example 1: Caching Effect

A poorly designed sql statement requires 100,000 disk reads. The designer is not aware of how poorly the code is written, since the report runs "okay." Normally, all the blocks are "cached up," so that the performance isn't too bad. The key is, good performance *requires* all the blocks to be cached. Even a small reduction in caching will have a disastrous effect.

Then, other jobs are added to the server, and the caching goes down from 99% to 90%. Suddenly, the report takes much longer. The users mistakenly search for the "proximate" cause, and ask, "What changed?" They don't realize that the code was poor to begin with.

Example 2: Unstable Execution Plans

In this case, the sql is overly complicated, with lots of bind variables and awkward joins. The optimizer struggles to figure out a good execution plan. Sometimes it gets it right, sometimes it doesn't. On the current server, given the current statistics and perceived bind variables, the optimizer has a decent plan, the sql runs well.

Now, the same code is run on another database. Stats are re-gathered, and new queries are run. This time, the code runs horribly. The users again ask, "What changed?" assuming that that question is a good place to start.

True Story: The Car Wash

A friend of mine took his car to the local car wash. The car came out nice and clean, but with just one problem: the windshield was cracked! Well, the car owner was mad, and demanded the car wash owner pay for the damage.

The owner of the car wash, being a former Oracle DBA and regular reader of this blog, refused to accept liability for the damage. He argued, *"Our car wash was only the proximate cause--not the ultimate cause."*

Well, okay, the car wash owner didn't really use the term, "proximate cause," but he understood the principle. The car wash owner suggested the windshield must have already been damaged, since many tens of thousands of cars had been processed over the years without causing any such damage.

The car wash was being blamed just because it was the *nearest* cause, not actually the root cause.

Lessons Learned

I am reluctant to begin any investigation with "What changed." A good DBA normally has far better methods to use.

Lesson #1: You Don't Really Know What Changed

Folks mean well, but rarely does anyone really know *for a fact* what has changed and what hasn't. How often do people say, "We haven't changed anything," but really can't guarantee that.

Lesson #2: Some Things *Always* Change

Even when a database is cloned to another server, many things will soon be different, even when everyone says, "We haven 't changed anything."

For example, the bind variables specified will usually be different. How the optimizer assesses the bind variables can also change. Here's another: The caching effect will always be different, depending on recent jobs run. When a user claims the report being run is identical as before, they cannot really know that for a fact.

Lesson #3: Poor Design Can Yield Varying Performance

You can write terrible sql, and sometimes you get away with it; the optimizer happens to get it right in your particular case. The problem is, it's an unstable solution, and can easily shift to a bad solution. The slightest change--such as stats, how bind variables are used, size of objects, or caching can trigger plan changes and miserable results.

It would be easy to get caught up analyzing all the factors that cause plan changes, but they are not relevant to the root cause.

We can Do Much Better

By looking for "What has changed," you are aiming at the wrong target. By focusing on recent events, you are actually analyzing the consequence of the bad design, not isolating the bad design itself.

Of course, I must admit, you can sometimes guess the right cause, but the "What's Changed" method is not a consistently good approach. We can do much better. DBAs have excellent ways to find root cause.

START #10 *QUANTIFY* THE PROBLEM

The Oracle Detective, once he or she has successfully *confirmed* the performance problem, should assign some numbers to the problem. Quantifying the problem is critical, and helps us in these ways:

✓ Numbers indicate the actual severity of the problem
✓ Numbers of the 'was condition' will be used later to illustrate the improvement
✓ Numbers give us a feel for how much effort should be expended

Sometimes, after the problem has been quantified, there is a consensus that the whole issue is simply "not worth the time." In other words, the problem may be deemed so trivial, that no further action is warranted.

For instance, if a "problem" SQL statement only requires a small fraction of a second to execute, it is not clear that anyone should spend time improving the execution time. (Of course, if that SQL statement is executed *millions* of times, then the effort should certainly be expended.)

Frequently, however, the quantification step reveals that the problem is *even worse than expected*. In either case, once the quantitative numbers are gathered, the performance expert will know the true magnitude of the problem, and can plan his effort accordingly.

Questions to ask

When quantifying the problem, there are several key areas to investigate. Some questions that the Oracle Detective should consider include:

✓ What is the elapsed time of the query?
✓ What is the CPU time consumed?
✓ How many disk reads are performed?
✓ How many logical reads are performed?
✓ How many times was the SQL statement executed?
✓ Is there a large network transfer?
✓ Is there any other server activity? If so, what and when?
✓ Are there other processes blocking the job?

START #11 LOOK FOR THE "HEAVY HITTERS"

I use this script to find those SQL queries that are responsible for the "slow database."

```
Select Executions, Buffer_Gets, Disk_Reads,
Sql_Text
From V$Sql
Where Disk_Reads/(.01+Executions) > 100000
Order By First_Load_Time
```

When we run the "heavy hitters" script, we are really making a certain assumption. We are suggesting that the database is not slow in some *general* sense, but in a very *specific* sense. This script does not tell us what is wrong in general—it tells us what is wrong *specifically*.

In a way, we are thinking (to ourselves) that the users are really in error—the database is not just "generally slow" at all—it is slow in some very specific ways. Recall one of our earlier axioms:

"Database problems are frequently reported inaccurately."

Of course, you can modify the script to not just look for heavy disk activity, but for large number of logical reads. I often run something like this, which finds the sql doing a lot of gets for each execution:

```
Select Executions, Buffer_Gets, Disk_Reads,
Sql_Text
From V$Sql
Where elapsed_time > 999999999
and buffer_gets/(.01+rows_processed) > 999999
Order By First_Load_Time
```

Naturally, you will want to customize each script to match your own situation. Perhaps you will want to include sql with a smaller elapsed time.

START #12 PROBLEMS OFTEN DUE TO *NON-TECHNICAL* REASONS

Don't assume that a huge performance crisis is due to some complicated reason. That is often not the case.

When you first analyze a problem, it is quite possible that the solution is so trivial, you can't understand how it was ever missed. You might hesitate to even mention the obvious cause, because it just seems too trivial.

For example, the root cause could be missing stats on the most important table in the database, forgetting to add a key index—or something equally simple. I have seen this happen countless times.

These types of problems happen because of some oversight, a step that was forgotten, or some other lapse. The reason the problem exists in the first place is often due to a poor process--not due to the great complexity of the performance problem.

It's not that the DBAs are too dim-witted to understand the importance of stats—it's just that no one thought to add that step to the process. Or maybe it's because a key DBA just quit the company.

Of course, this does not mean that Oracle technology is not involved. The tuning process will certainly require technical analysis and troubleshooting, and the solution will likely require some technical modification.

Fixing a Production Problem

These types of oversights happen *all the time*—even on production systems. Performance problems on production systems are often as simple to resolve as problems on development systems.

The main difference in resolving issues in production, is that management is quite a bit more excited and motivated to do something this time. Also, there is greater complexity in testing the solution, since significant changes cannot just be "thrown into" an important production database.

START #13 BUILD A TRUSTING RELATIONSHIP

A performance analyst who has successfully established a position of trust will go very far. He won't have to look for clients—they will seek *him* out

One TV commercial shown recently asks, "Wouldn't it be great if you could trust your broker?" Well, this is the same sort of question that IT managers ask: "Wouldn't it be great if you could trust your DBA?"

The reality is, that there are not too many Oracle performance analysts who have earned the trust of their clients. Some Oracle analysts are technically savvy, but alienate their co-workers with their abrasive personality. Others are very "nice," but are not really technically competent. That is why the Oracle analyst who can combine *both* traits—the art and the science--has a *huge* career advantage.

Your PROBLEM is Important to Me

The inductive approach to performance tuning—which I call the *"Physician-to-Magician"* approach will act like a catalyst to building trusting relationships. In fact, the entire approach is based on the principle of *putting the needs of our customers first.*

A genuine act of listening gives the customer the tacit message, "I think your problem is important." On the other hand, the database analyst who fails to seriously listen to his "patients" also gives the client a message—"Your problems are not very important to me." This type of analyst will not do nearly as well as the analyst who takes his client's problems seriously.

A Big Career Boost

For those interested in advancing their career, these are very relevant observations, with huge career implications. In the medical world, the doctor who truly sympathizes with the problems of his patients will have a booming practice. Similarly, the performance expert who is *competent as well as empathetic* will have many firms vying for his or her skills.

BLUNDERS TO AVOID

I have encountered a wide variety of big blunders. And some of them I have made myself! Check out the mistakes listed here.

"I Forgot to Gather Stats?"

BLUNDER #1 USING WRONG TUNING APPROACH

The DBA will often encounter various obstacles during the treatment process. For instance, users may tire of complaining. Rather than informing the DBA of performance issues, they decide to live with problems rather than report them. In this case, the DBA simply remains ignorant of the problem.

Sometimes the application designers will resist divulging poor performance. This occurs because investigation might reveal poor or embarrassing design techniques.

Along with obstacles to jump, the DBA may fall into several traps. Here are some common pitfalls that I have seen:

Assuming a solution

Rather than perform the labor to identify the true root cause, it is tempting to skip the analysis and jump right to the solution. This frequently manifests itself by the premature purchase of bigger/better hardware.

Looking for exotic solutions

Another way to jump to the conclusion is to implement more complex, or "exotic" changes. For instance: assuming that raw disk partitions are the solution, or changing the value of the spin_count parameter.

Looking for the magic parameter

It is tempting to believe that a simple change to an init.ora parameter will solve the performance problems. This is usually a vain hope.

Ignoring application design

It is extremely common for a defective application/database design to be hindering proper performance.

Blaming the user

This is an especially attractive option; it has the added benefit that the user is usually not present to defend himself.

BLUNDER #2 BLAMING THE USER

With the Physician-to-Magician approach to performance tuning, it is important that you gain the trust of your database customers—whether they are the actual end users, designers, or programmers. This step is critical, because by gaining the users' confidence, the job of the performance expert actually becomes easier. Serious problems will be avoided, performance on the production system will likely be wonderful, and everyone on the team (including the DBA, of course) ends up looking like a genius.

With a trusting relationship between the DBA and designers, problems are solved much earlier. For instance, instead of producing a questionable design and quickly sending it into production, the developer will consult with the DBA, or even ask the DBA to look over the preliminary design.

The designers will do this because they believe that the DBA will *help* them, not *blame* them. With this trust, poor preliminary designs are corrected before they become poor *final* designs. Also, the DBA will be informed of possible performance bottlenecks *before* they go into production.

In order to gain this trust, the DBA must avoid blaming the designer when performance is lacking, or a really poor design has been implemented. Instead of blame, the DBA can choose to *assist* the designer by focusing on the *problem*, not the person. This allows the designer to be part of the *solution*, rather than part of the *problem*. Almost anyone would cooperate on these terms.

Share The Credit For Solving Performance Problems

In contrast to this, if the designer is always getting "blamed," or senses a hostile or accusatory tone in the DBA, he will simply choose to "go around" the DBA whenever possible. After all, no one wants to get blamed for a problem; no one wants to be yelled at. Everyone wants to be recognized for making a good contribution.

BLUNDER #3 BLAMING INSUFFICIENT RESOURCES

This tactic is especially common, and it's so easy to do! If you don't know what to do, you can always say, "Add memory!" or "Add more CPU's!" It's easy to say, because it requires no analysis. And that's part of the fun--anybody, no matter how incompetent, can make that suggestion.

The value of this suggestion matches the work required to produce it. It is rarely the right answer. Performance suggestions that rely on generalities are rarely the answer. Specific performance problems require specific performance solutions. Considering all the performance problems I have analyzed, only a handful of performance problems were due to insufficient memory or CPUs.

> *I've never actually seen even one performance problem that was due to insufficient database cache. (A friend of mine told me he saw one once.)*

Normally, if some people are determined to add more memory to the database cache, I don't argue with them, but just continue on analyzing the real problem. After all, it won't hurt anything to have more memory. We did a test recently on a 100 TB database (which already had plenty of memory.) By drastically increasing the database buffers, we attained a 1% improvement in the cache "hit ratio."

Of course, if you are in the early stages of creating some application and setting up the database, you might indeed discover that you need to change some init.ora parameters. As part of the design process, you may discover you have grossly underestimated the CPU requirements.

Usually, however, the siren call for more CPU or memory is based on guesswork, not actual analysis by experienced DBAs.

BLUNDER #4 HAVING A POMPOUS ATTITUDE

In order to foster a trusting relationship, it is important that all parties avoid a *pompous attitude*. We have all been on project teams that have certain "dysfunctional" members, who must always "get their way." From sheer force of personality, these individuals often force the team to follow their recommendations. Many engineers, being introverts by nature, will opt to avoid a confrontation, and simply go along with the recommendation, rather than make it an issue.

Even just one or two "swollen heads" on a team can completely destroy a team's chemistry. Instead of working in a spirit of cooperation, meetings tend to be exercises in defending one's position, or justifying past work. Outside the meeting, programmers will do their job grudgingly. Instead of feeling that they are making a contribution, team players are reduced to the position of "order takers."

This type of situation is the opposite of trust. A pompous attitude really says to everyone else on the team, "You are not important. There is no reason to listen to your ideas." Obviously, a team with this chemistry will be at a huge disadvantage. Instead of benefiting from the minds of many people, with various backgrounds, the project degrades into just one man's design.

DBAs are some of the smartest people I know—really! Is it possible that sometimes our head gets a little swollen out of proportion? Our next case study illustrates how one pompous individual was able to seriously impede a project, and create discord in an entire department.

BLUNDER #5 RELYING ON CACHE "HIT RATIO"

Historically, many DBAs have taken the data cache hit ratio as an important figure of merit, bragging about how close to 100% their ratio is. Their reasoning is that a good hit ratio is desirable; thus, a very high ratio must really be great!

What is wrong with this reasoning? After all, isn't it better to have most reads accomplished through logical I/O instead of physical I/O?

The answer is, yes, it is better, all *things being equal.* The problem is, high cache hit ratios are sometimes achieved by performing certain operations that achieve excellent hit ratios at the cost of highly inflated logical reads. Specifically, improper use of indexes will often drive the cache-hit ratio extremely high. This happens because the index blocks are typically all (or mostly) cached. Since the database uses blocks that are exclusive cached, it gets "credit" for using them.

Of course, the real question is, should the Oracle engine be using that execution plan? Is it the most efficient in terms of *all* resources? In certain situations, a very impressive cache hit ratio is actually an indication of a *poorly* tuned database!

Thus, the Oracle tuning expert should not be obsessed with the cache-hit ratio. Instead, the analyst must be sure to consider the amount of logical I/O as well. Driving down logical I/O will also tend to drive down physical I/O.

BLUNDER #6 FOOLED BY DISPLAY OF HUGE RESULT SET

In some cases, a query returns so many rows that the time to *display* the rows becomes the driving factor for the total execution time. This makes it difficult to distinguish between actual database-related time and the time to display the result set. When running the query in Sql*Plus, the long display time will likely mask the underlying problem, or exaggerate the actual run time.

There are several ways around this difficulty. One simple way is to reword the SQL code to insert the results into a temporary table, rather than actually displaying the results.

For example, consider a large query that returns 10,000 rows. (Assume for this example that indexes are not being used). Note how the SQL could be rewritten to facilitate a simple timing test:

```
Select Emp_Number
From Dept
Where Emp_Number > 100;
```

Can be re-written as:

```
Insert into Temp_Tab
(
Select Emp_Number
From Dept
Where Emp_Number > 100
);
```

A possible disadvantage with the above approach is that when Sql*Plus *Autotrace* is being used to display the execution plan, the "Insert" method will prevent the execution plan from being shown. The *Timing* function in Sql*Plus will still function, however.

An alternative way to achieve the same result is to modify the *Select* clause to specify a *function* rather than the raw data. Instead of returning each row, we simply force the optimizer to fetch each row *as though* it is going to be displayed. The execution plan will normally remain the same, and

Sql*Plus *Autotrace* will work fine. Continuing with our same example, this is how the SQL text could be reworded:

Original SQL:

```
Select Emp_Number
From Dept
Where Emp_Number > 100;
```

Can be rewritten as:

```
Select Max  (Emp_Number)
From Dept
Where Emp_Number > 100;
```

By using the function *Max*, there is little change to the work that the Oracle engine will have to perform. The Oracle engine will still have to retrieve exactly the same rows as before; the only difference is that they will not be *displayed*. (Admittedly, there will be a very slight impact due to the new function, but this effect is usually negligible—especially when compared to the magnitude of the performance problem being investigated.)

When simplifying a SQL query to use the function approach, be careful to not disturb the execution plan. For instance, if certain fields are *removed* from the *Select* clause, the optimizer may modify the execution plan to take advantage of the lessened requirement. For instance, with fields removed from the Select clause, an *index* access might retrieve all the information needed, when a table access was required before. When in doubt, compare the execution plans for the two SQL statements.

BLUNDER #7 FOOLED BY THE CACHE EFFECT

When performing sample runtime tests, remember that the second and subsequent queries will usually be much faster because the majority of data fetched will likely be cached. Don't be fooled into believing that some slight change has "fixed" the problem, when nothing has been corrected at all. I have seen designers fooled many times by this.

In one particular case I worked, the designer was led to believe that a certain SQL query was really well tuned; in reality, the subsequent reports had merely taken advantage of caching much of the data. The number of physical I/Os was substantially reduced (at least for the artificial setup in the testing environment); nevertheless, the huge number of logical I/Os was not reduced at all. Eventually, the SQL was tuned to eliminate the logical I/Os as well.

Don't forget that the SAN disk system will also cache the data; this effect may even be more significant than the database caching. It will be tough to remove this effect, even if you are able to eliminate the database caching. On numerous occasions, junior DBAs have told me that they eliminated the caching effect (for example by restarting the instance.) In each case, they didn't realize that the SAN still had the data cached up.

Because of caching, the number of physical reads can vary greatly in runs that take place close in time. That's a good reason to focus on the *logical* work done by Oracle, rather than counting the exact number of disk reads.

BLUNDER #8 WRONG USE OF PARALLELISM

Mistakes in parallelism may be the biggest problem I encounter. Many queries submitted for performance analysis have *Parallel* hints, but the efficiency of the sql--which is far more important, has been neglected.

This predicament is common, because it's easy to add a *Parallel* hint, but it takes skill and time to make the sql efficient. Invoking parallelism disguises the inefficiency sometimes, since a ton of parallel processes can often (if only temporarily) cover-up the problem with the sql. Oracle can perform a full scan of a typical billion-row table in just a few minutes using Parallel 6 (of course, the actual fields in the table have a big effect.)

> *I have found a good rule of thumb is limiting the parallelism to 6 or 8, except for extreme cases (such as rebuilding a monstrous index when you have the entire system to yourself.)*

It's true that degrees beyond 6 or 8 provide some improvement, but the benefit falls-off, as you consume more resources. Then, those resources are not available to other jobs. If you do use parallelism, be sure to specify the degree; do not let Oracle decide how many processes to invoke--it could be way more than you expect.

BLUNDER #9 SETTING PARALLELISM AT THE TABLE LEVEL

The problem is that you lose control over exactly when parallelism is used. If you set parallelism at the table or index level, Oracle will attempt to start parallel processes anytime you include the table in your query. This means that you will be taking away resources that might have been better used servicing other transactions and queries.

Depending on the exact sql, the parallel processes may not actually begin, but why take the chance? In actuality, you probably only wanted parallelism for a specific type of query—not for *all* queries on that table.

Here is an easy way to see if parallelism is set at the table level:

```
Select Table_Name, Degree
from Dba_Tables
where Degree not like '%1%';
```

And to check indexes:

```
Select Index_Name, Degree
from Dba_Indexes
where Degree not like '%1%';
```

This is very common with indexes. Very often, after rebuilding an index in parallel, the DBA will forget to reset the index back to Noparallel. I have done this myself more than once.

BLUNDER #10 SQL HINT MISTAKES

Although SQL hints are amazingly effective, simply adding a hint to the SQL statement does *not* guarantee that the optimizer will "obey" the hint. In most cases, it is not a "bug" in Oracle that is preventing the hint from working; instead, the problem is most likely due to:

- Wrong hint syntax, such as *comma* instead of *space*
- Referring to non-existent object (i.e., incorrect table or index name)
- Using the table *name* rather than the table *alias*.

Remember the funny rule about SQL hints: When an alias is used in the original SQL, then the alias must likewise be specified in the SQL hint. Observe the hint syntax for the following SQL, which correctly specifies the hint USE_NL to use a nested loop:

```
SELECT /*+Use_NL (C D) */
Cust_Name
From Customer C, Department D
WHERE C.Cust_Id = D.Cust_Id
AND Dept_Name = 'Engineering';
```

The SQL above correctly uses the two table aliases—C and D. Observe also the allowable mix of case. Even with a mix of upper and lower case in the hint, the optimizer will accept the above statement.

Unfortunately, incorrect syntax in a hint will not always be easy to discover. Many analysts and DBAs have spent hours wondering why the optimizer is not "obeying" the hint, only to later discover some typo in the hint syntax. In case of wrong syntax or "typos," the optimizer will simply ignore the hint--but you will never be told!

Be sure to put the SQL hint immediately after the *Select* (or *Delete*, etc.) key word. Putting some other words after Select will invalidate the hint. Consider the following SQL, slightly modified from above (keyword *Distinct* added). The SQL as written below contains a serious error that will prevent the hint from being accepted:

WRONG:

```
Select Distinct /*+Use_NL (C D) */
Cust_Name
From Customer C, Department D
Where C.Cust_Id = D.Cust_Id
And Dept_Name = 'Engineering';
```

Did you spot it? Of course, it is the word *Distinct* that has been (incorrectly) positioned between *Select* and the SQL hint. When this SQL is run, the optimizer will not "balk" at running the SQL; it simply ignores the hint!

Here is the right way to include the *distinct* keyword:

RIGHT:

```
Select /*+Use_NL (C D) */
Distinct Cust_Name
From Customer C, Department D
Where C.Cust_Id = D.Cust_Id
And Dept_Name = 'Engineering';
```

Notice that the keyword Distinct has simply been moved after the SQL hint. This is the right way to formulate that SQL query.

BLUNDER #11 JUMPING TO INCREASE THE DATABASE BUFFER SIZE

The "increase the parameters" strategy has a certain appeal, because it sounds so logical and scientific. In this line of reasoning, performance problems will disappear as the cache hit ratio increases.

At first, this sounds logical since a high cache hit ratio means fewer disk reads. The grand fallacy with the "increase the buffer" strategy is that it fails to address the *root cause* of the problem. In the rush to achieve a solution, no time is spent calmly analyzing the facts and finding a root cause that matches the facts. That is, just like a "guessing" strategy, a sound process is not even considered as the analyst hopes to find a solution that doesn't require any real work.

This approach is nothing more than guessing. The problem with guessing is that there are unlimited number of guesses one can make. If you ask around the office, everyone can make a guess, no matter their competence in the subject matter.

Of course, it won't do any harm to increase the database cache size, but it's a big distraction. Whenever anyone suggests this approach, I ask, "So, that's the root cause of the problem?"

EASY & POWERFUL SCRIPTS

In this section I have provided some of the most powerful scripts I use. I hope you find them as helpful as I do.

SCRIPT #1 FIND SQL USING STORED OUTLINES OR PROFILES

I often want to see exactly which sql are being affected by a stored outline. Here is an easy way to get that information:

```
Col Ol_Name format a10
Col Category format a12
Col timestamp format a25

Select /*+PARALLEL(X 8) */
Ol_Name, Category, Timestamp,
SQL_TEXT
From Outln.Ol$ X
WHERE CATEGORY = 'MY_CATEGORY'
Order By Timestamp;
```

Similarly, to see which sql is using a sql profile, you can run something like this script:

```
Select First_Load_Time, Inst_Id,
Sql_Id, Executions,
Round(Elapsed_Time/1000000) Secs, Sql_Text
From Gv$Sql
Where Sql_Profile Is Not Null
And Last_Active_Time > Sysdate - .1
Order By Last_Active_Time;
```

SCRIPT #2 EASY WAY TO SEE BIND VARIABLES

I use two scripts to find the contents of a bind variable. One script from the V$ views, and one from the Dba_Hist tables.

First, the one from V$Sqlarea:

```
Select distinct a.inst_ID,
to_char(last_captured, 'mon-dd-hh24:mi') cap,
c.name||'/'||c.value_string bind_var,
datatype, datatype_string
from GV$sqlarea a,
dba_users b,
gv$sql_bind_capture c
where b.user_id=a.parsing_user_id
and b.username != 'SYS'
and c.address=a.address
AND a.sql_id = tbd
order by 1,2;
```

Here's a list of the historical bind variables sampled for each Snap:

```
Select snap_id, position, last_captured,
a.value_string bind_var,
datatype_string
from dba_hist_sqlbind a
where a.sql_id = tbd
order by 1,2,3;
```

Keep in mind that these are *sampled* bind variables. That is, you aren't really guaranteed to get the variable for any particular iteration of that exact Sql. Nevertheless, I've find these to be useful to get an idea of typical binds used.

SCRIPT #3 MONITOR ACTIVE SESSIONS

I use this script all the time. You can join the views V$Session and V$Sql. There are many different possibilities for field selection—here is one example:

```
Col SText format a50

Select DISTINCT Sid, Username,
Substr(Sql_Text,1,200) Stext
From V$Session, V$Sql
Where Status = 'ACTIVE'
And Username Is Not Null
And V$Session.Sql_Hash_Value = Hash_Value
And V$Session.Sql_Address  = V$Sql.Address
And Sql_Text Not Like '%Sql_Text%'
And Username <> 'SYS';
```

In the above query, we eliminate the SYS user because we don't want to clutter up the output with information about the Oracle background processes. Also, we exclude Sql that includes the phrase, "Sql_Text" because otherwise this very Sql will show up as active.

Note: I've observed that this script runs a lot slower in Oracle 12c, compared to prior database versions. So, I often use my RAC "Sessions" script instead, which shows all activity on all nodes. (See the RAC hints.)

What does "Active" Mean?

Active does *not* just mean that the user is connected to Oracle. It means that the session is actively doing work *at that very moment*. For example, an active session is oftentimes doing disk I/O, but that is not the only reason to be active.

Very often, especially on OLTP systems, such as customer service applications, nearly all of the sessions are *inactive*. This simply reflects the fact that most of the user's time is spent doing something else, such as talking to a customer on the phone, or typing in a request. The actual database request usually completes in a fraction of a second.

SCRIPT #4 TRACK HISTORICAL DISK READS

I sometimes want to see if there is unusual disk read activity, at certain times of the day. Or, after making a big performance fix, I want to confirm that the disk reads have dropped way down.

Here is an easy way to list the total physical reads in your database, sorted by snapshot id. If the pattern is not obvious, I will often copy the results into a spreadsheet, and chart the results.

In the script below, I only include times that have more than 5,000 disk reads:

```
Select S.Snap_Id,
To_Char(Begin_Interval_Time, 'Dd-Mon-Yy-Hh24:Mi')
Time_Start,
Round(Sum(Physical_Reads_Delta)/1000000)
Meg_Block_Reads
From Dba_Hist_Seg_Stat D
, Dba_Hist_Snapshot S
Where S.Snap_Id = D.Snap_Id
And S.Instance_Number = D.Instance_Number
Group By S.Snap_Id,
To_Char(Begin_Interval_Time, 'Dd-Mon-Yy-Hh24:Mi')
Having  Sum(Physical_Reads_Delta) > 5000
Order By 1,2
```

SNAP_ID	TIME_START	MEG_BLOCK_READS
7718	19-feb-18-02:00	3
7720	19-feb-18-04:00	6
7721	19-feb-18-05:00	4
7724	19-feb-18-08:00	1
7725	19-feb-18-09:00	1
7726	19-feb-18-10:00	2
7727	19-feb-18-11:00	1
7729	19-feb-18-13:00	2

SCRIPT #5 ESTIMATING LONG QUERIES: 3 WAYS

How often has a user asked, "How long until my job finishes?" If the sql is doing full scans, there are a few ways to estimate the runtime.

Method 1: OEM

Oracle Enterprise Manager (OEM) has a very nice graphic that shows progress of big table scans.

Method 2: Query "Longsops" View

Behind the scenes, OEM is actually querying a view called *V$Session_Longops*. Here is one possible way to query the view:

```
Select Sid, Message from V$Session_Longops
where Sid = tbd;

  SID MESSAGE
----- ------------------------------------------
 2057 Table Scan:CHRIS.TABLEX: 926717 out of
      926717  Blocks done
```

Here's a slight different way to accomplish the same thing:

```
Select Sid, Time_Remaining, Elapsed_Seconds
from V$Session_Longops where Sid = 123;

  SID TIME_REMAINING ELAPSED_SECONDS
----- --------------- ---------------
  123              11              58
```

Method 3:

Actually, I never use the *V$Session_Longops* table. Instead, I do this:

- In the sql being run, note the tables that need to be scanned
- Get the table size (blocks) from Dba_Segments
- Query V$Sql to get the Disk_Reads performed so far.

You can easily watch the progress of your sql, and compare the blocks read so far, to the total blocks in the tables.

SCRIPT #6 IDENTIFY UNUSED INDEXES

You can use *index monitoring*. Oracle provides a monitoring facility whereby you can see if an index is ever used during the monitoring period. The command to start monitoring is really simple. For instance, if we want to monitor the index *Chris1*, we run the following:

```
Alter Index Chris1 Monitoring Usage;
```

After several days (or weeks), check the results by running:

```
Select Index_Name, Table_Name, Used
From V$Object_Usage;
```

INDEX_NAME	TABLE_NAME	USED
CHRIS1	CHRISTEST	NO

To turn off monitoring, simply run:

```
Alter Index Chris1 Nomonitoring Usage;
```

While useful, this simple "Yes"/"No" answer for each index checked is not that helpful. It would be much more useful to identify the exact SQL that used the index, along with the resource usage.

For example, Oracle might be using a certain index only because you haven't given it any better alternatives. Just because the index is used, doesn't mean it's a good choice. By knowing statistics such as elapsed time or disk I/O, you can identify tuning opportunities.

SCRIPT #7 SPOT "ITL" LOCKING

ITL stands for *Interested Transaction List*. This type of locking occurs when many sessions are trying to update the same block, but there is no more room in the header to account for more transactions. When ITL locking occurs, the latest transaction will wait until one of the earlier transactions commits or rolls back, thereby freeing up an ITL slot.

ITL locking is a bit rare, but occasionally happens—usually in environments running complex batch jobs. When this occurs it can be extremely frustrating, since the symptoms closely resemble row-level locking.

Several things have to happen at the same time to get an ITL lock:

- Multiple sessions try to update the exact same block
- There are no more ITL slots in the header block
- There is no spare room in the data block to allow header to expand (i.e., the block is jammed full.)

Oracle typically reserves two ITL slots in the block header. This is configurable, and is controlled by the parameter, *Initrans*, set when the table is first created.

You can detect ITL waits in your database by querying the view, *V$Segment_Statistics*. Here's one example:

```
Select Owner,
Object_Name||' '||Subobject_Name Object_Name,
Value
From V$Segment_Statistics
Where Statistic_Name = 'ITL waits'
And Value > 0
Order By 3,1,2;
```

SCRIPT #8 IDENTIFY OBJECT BEING READ BY A CERTAIN SESSION

The easiest way, available since Oracle 9i, is to query the *V$Sql* view and look for the column *Dba_Object_Id*. You join that to Dba_Objects to get the table (or index) name.

Here's one possibility, which shows the username, the sql being run, and the actual object name currently being read:

```
Select DISTINCT Osuser, Sid, Username,
Substr(Program,1,19) PROG, Object_Name,
Sql_Text
From V$Session, V$Sql, Dba_Objects O
Where V$Session.Status = 'ACTIVE'
And Username Is Not Null
And O.Object_Id = Row_Wait_Obj#
And V$Session.Sql_Hash_Value = Hash_Value
And V$Session.Sql_Address  = V$Sql.Address
And Username <> 'SYS';
```

In the above sql, I eliminate Sys users, since I'm typically interested in regular users, not some DBA (or background) activity.

Another valid way (but much more cumbersome), is to use wait events. Using *V$Session_Wait* and the p1,p2,p3 parameters, you first determine the file number and block. You then figure out what object matches that file/block combination. This older method works, but of course takes much longer. (This second method applies only to reading from *disk*.)

SCRIPT #9 SHOW RESOURCES USED BY A SESSION

If the session is your *own* session, than you can use the view, *V$Mystat*. This view includes cumulative values for many different actions:

```
Select Name, Value
From V$Mystat One, V$Statname Two
Where One.Statistic# = Two.Statistic#
And Value > 50000;
```

```
NAME                                    VALUE
----------------------------------   --------
physical read total bytes              237568
physical read bytes                    237568
```

If the statistics are for some *other* session, you can use the view, *V$sesstat*:

```
Select Sid, Name, Value From V$Sesstat One,
V$Statname Two
Where Sid = 592
And One.Statistic# = Two.Statistic#
And Value > 5000000;
```

```
SID NAME                                          VALUE
----- ----------------------------------------   ----------
592 physical read total bytes                  273842176
592 physical read bytes                        273842176
```

In the above sql, we just wanted to see activity exceeding a certain threshold. You will likely want to exclude some resource usage—perhaps things like connect time, or bytes transferred over Sql*net. Of course, we could have instead focused on some particular resource. For example, we could show physical i/o using this:

```
Select Sid, Name, Value From V$Sesstat One,
V$Statname Two
Where Sid = 592
And One.Statistic# = Two.Statistic#
And Upper(Name) like '%PHYSICAL READS';
```

SCRIPT #10 IDENTIFY OBJECTS WITH MOST LOGICAL & PHYSICAL READS

Of course, this information is available in AWR reports. If you don't have these reports available, one easy way is to query the view, *V$Segment_Statistics.*

Here is one example for finding objects with huge logical I/O:

```
Select Owner,Statistic_Name,
Object_Name||' '||Subobject_Name Object_Name,
Value
From V$Segment_Statistics
Where Statistic_Name Like '%logical reads%'
And Value > 333000000
Order By 4,2,3;
```

OWNER	STATISTIC_NAME	OBJECT_NAME	VALUE
CHRIS	logical reads	TEST_TABLE	368389216

Here's an example for physical reads:

```
Select Owner,Statistic_Name,
Object_Name||' '||Subobject_Name Object_Name,
Value
From V$Segment_Statistics
Where Statistic_Name Like '%physical reads%'
And Value > 333000000
Order By 4,2,3;
```

OWNER	STATISTIC_NAME	OBJECT_NAME	VALUE
CHRIS	physical reads	TEST_TABLE	561526416

Naturally, you will customize your query to fit your own system.

SCRIPT #11 ESTIMATE THE *SEQUENTIAL READ RATE*

Single block reads are typically performed at rates above 100/sec. On many systems, the rate can be above 200 seq reads/sec. This means a latency between 5 and 10 ms.

Naturally, you will want to know the particular rate on your system. There are several good ways to do this. In the AWR report, sequential reads are listed. Very often, sequential reads will be listed as part of the "Top 5 Timed Events."

Even if sequential reads are not a "top 5" event, this information will be listed, along with all wait events, in the "Wait Event" section. In this section, the average wait (ms) is shown. Simply take the reciprocal to get the read rate.

Besides reports, you can easily estimate the rate achievable (for a single thread) by querying a view such as *V$FileStat*, or *V$System_Event*. Here's one possibility:

```
Select EVENT, TOTAL_WAITS,  TIME_WAITED ,
Round(100*Total_Waits/Time_Waited) Rate
From V$System_Event
Where Event Like 'db file sequential read%';

EVENT                    TOTAL_WAITS TIME_WAITED     RATE
------------------------ ----------- ----------- --------
db file sequential read   6232709774   226760222      274
```

Note that the rate above is an estimate of what a *single* thread could reasonably achieve.

Another possibility is to examine the appropriate wait event in a tkprof output. This will not be as accurate, however, since the listing shows the wait times just for the particular session being traced, rather than an overall rate for a long period of time.

SCRIPT #12 FIND THE EXECUTION PATH THAT WAS *ACTUALLY RUN*

This question is not as trivial as it may appear. The key here is understanding that the results of an *Explain Plan* are not necessarily the same as the plan *actually run*. Of course, the vast majority of times, the explain plan is very accurate—but not always!

The execution plan that was actually run in the database is available in the view, *V$Sql_Plan*. You can query this table just like the usual Plan_Table. The difference is, that you identify the sql a little differently.

Here's one way to do it: First, find the address for the sql in question. This is listed in the view, *V$Sql*. Then, simply query V$Sql_Plan using that address.

Here's an example:

```
Select Cost, Object_Name, Operation, Options
From V$Sql_Plan
Where Address = '00000005fc1e1998';
```

COST	OBJECT_NAME	OPERATION	OPTIONS
31		SELECT STATEMENT	
		COUNT	STOPKEY
31		VIEW	
31		SORT	ORDER BY STOPKEY
30		PARTITION RANGE	ALL
30	EMP_HIST	TABLE ACCESS	BY LOCAL INDEX ROWID
29	EMP_IDX1	INDEX	RANGE SCAN

SCRIPT #13 EASY WAY TO SEE THE P1, P2, P3 PARAMETERS

It is important to understand what these parameters mean. These are *wait event parameters*. When using Oracle's wait event facility, they provide extra information for the particular wait event.

For example, here's a sql to retrieve the sequential read wait event—probably one of the most common wait events.

```
Select Sid, Event, P1, P2, P3
From V$Session_Wait
Where Event Like '%db file seq%';

 SID EVENT                    P1         P2         P3
----- ------------------- ------- ---------- ----------
 1998 db file sequential    12     564683         1
  821 db file sequential    12     403592         1
```

In the sql above, P1 represents the file#, P2 represents the block id, and P3 indicates how many Oracle blocks were read. Of course, the P1-P3 parameters have different interpretations for different wait events.

Note that the event names are listed in *V$Event_Name*.

SCRIPT #14 SEE HOW MANY DISK READS FOR A SQL STATEMENT

There's several ways to accomplish this. Probably the easiest (and fastest) way is to simply look at the view, *V$Sql*, and examine the column *Disk_Reads*. Here's an example:

```
Select Executions EXEC, Buffer_Gets GETS,
Disk_Reads IO, Sql_Text
From V$Sql
Where Upper(Sql_Text) Like '%EMP_TABLE%';

  EXEC    GETS      IO SQL_TEXT
------- ------- ------- --------------------------
     2       2      99 Select * from Emp_Table
```

We should note that this V$Sql view provides *cumulative* statistics. Therefore, if more than one user is running the identical sql, the results will be larger than for just a single user.

Of course, the same statistical information is also available in the Statspack and AWR reports, but it's often faster to just query V$Sql to get the same information.

Another way is to trace a session, then review the trace output; however, I rarely find that necessary. Why would I trace a session when the information is so easily obtainable?

SCRIPT #15 HOW TO SPOT EXCESSIVE *LOG FILE SYNC*

This is the delay due to writing the redo log buffers to disk. A lot of time spent waiting on log sync may be indicative of a design flaw—that is, excessive commits, but it may also indicate slow disks. In some cases, a high commit frequency simply reflects the true business requirements of the application. There is nothing inherently wrong with frequent commits—as long as they reflect the true business requirement.

For systems with excessive commits, this wait event will be listed in the AWR report. Use this information to see how often you perform log file sync, as well as the *latency*. Here is an example, which happens to include log file sync as the #5 top wait event.

```
Top 5 Timed Events

                                                    % Total
Event                         Waits     Time (s) Ela Time
--------------------------  ----------  --------  --------
db file sequential read     3,610,988    13,969    68.52
CPU time                                  4,553    22.33
ARCH wait on SENDREQ              789       733     3.60
db file parallel write        28,031       270     1.32
log file sync                 50,837       213     1.04
```

For the period measured by the above report, the system performed 50,837 syncs, and the potential rate (i.e., for a single thread) is about $50837/213 = 238$ writes/sec. Alternatively, here is a way to estimate the rate on your system:

```
Select Event, Total_Waits,  Time_Waited ,
Round(100*Total_Waits/Time_Waited) Rate
From V$System_Event
Where Event Like '%log file sync%';

EVENT             TOTAL_WAITS TIME_WAITED      RATE
----------------  ----------- -----------  ----------
log file sync        28308678    28339804         100
```

For the system having the statistics shown above, a single session could perform about 100 log syncs per second.

SCRIPT #16 EXAMINE *CHANGES* TO THE SEQUENTIAL READ RATE

I have long monitored the single-block (in Oracle-ease, "Sequential") read rate. I have found this to be an excellent metric—perhaps my #1 metric. You can easily summarize this metric by querying gv$System_Event, and looking for "db file sequential read."

To get valuable information, we're going to use *Dba_Hist_Filestatxs*. This contains disk i/o information, sorted by filename and Snap_id. For RAC systems, it also includes the *Instance_Number.*

Querying this table is a little tricky, because we need to get the "delta" information for a snapshot period—not the cumulative information.

Getting Precise Disk I/O

Using query subfactoring—the "with" syntax, we first find the total disk reads and time for a certain snapshot period and certain RAC node. This will make subsequent steps much simpler.

We'll call these metrics **Megreads** and **Ms** (milliseconds.) Of course, it's not really mandatory to use query subfactoring; I just like breaking things up into bite-sized chunks for easier debugging, and to make the query easier to understand:

```
With S1 as (Select Snap_Id,
Round(Sum(Singleblkrds)/1000000,1) Megreads,
Round(Sum(Singleblkrdtim)*10) Ms
From Dba_Hist_Filestatxs
Where Snap_Id > TBD
And Instance_Number = TBD
Group By Snap_Id);
```

Now let's change from cumulative to delta using the analytical function "lag" to go back just 1row, which for us really means go back 1 snapshot..

We use lag twice to get the delta values, **Totrds** and **Tot_Ms:**

```
S2 as ( Select
Snap_Id, Megreads - Lag(Megreads,1) Over(Order
By Snap_Id) Totrds,
Ms- Lag(Ms,1) Over (Order By Snap_Id) Tot_Ms
From S1 )
```

Finally, let's just do a simple calculation to get the metrics we really want. We really only want to see busy periods, so let's filter out periods with less than 1 million reads:

```
Select Snap_Id, Totrds Megards,
Round(Tot_Ms/Totrds/1000000,1) "Latency(Ms)"
From S2
Where Totrds > 1
```

Here's what the final query looks like.

```
With S1 As (
Select /*+Parallel(X 10) */ Snap_Id,
Round(Sum(Singleblkrds)/1000000,1)
Megreads, Round(Sum(Singleblkrdtim)*10) Ms
From Dba_Hist_Filestatxs X
Where Snap_Id > 35400 And Instance_Number In (3)
And Upper(Filename) Like '%DB0%' --optional
filter
Group By Snap_Id),
--
S2 As
(Select Snap_Id, Megreads - Lag(Megreads,1)
Over(Order By Snap_Id) Totrds,
Ms- Lag(Ms,1) Over (Order By Snap_Id) Tot_Ms
From S1 )
--
Select Snap_Id, Totrds Megards,
Round(Tot_Ms/Totrds/1000000,1)
"Latency(Ms)" From S2 Where Totrds > 1
```

Sometimes, I include a filter on certain file names, in case I'm analyzing reads on particular file systems. To speed things up, I generally use parallelism due to the large size of these tables on our system (especially monsters containing active session history.)

SCRIPT #17 FIND ACTIVE SESSIONS BY DATE

Very often, I hear of a problem report such as, "My report ran too long last night." The user will know the approximate start/end time, but will almost never know the node. (Plus, sometimes, various threads run on multiple nodes.)

One of the first scripts I run is a simple ASH script that categorizes the long-running sql by node, over a particular time period.

```
With P1 As (Select /*+Parallel(A 6) */
Distinct A.*
From Dba_Hist_Active_Sess_History A
Where Sample_Time Like '22-APR-10%4.%AM'
) Select Instance_Number, Sql_Id, Count(*)
From P1
Group By Instance_Number, Sql_Id
Having Count(*) > 20
Order By Count(*)
```

In the script above, I look for the activity, for all nodes, at 4 to 5 A.M. on April 22. I employ Parallel 6 to reduce the runtime due just a minute or so. I find it convenient to use query subfactoring (the "with" syntax), but of course that is not mandatory.

SCRIPT #18 SUMMARIZE DATABASE LOAD

If I suspect some drastic change in the database workload, I will run a script to summarize the workload over time. I find it convenient to use "Database Time Per Sec" for this metric. I generally use a filter so that I only show workload above a certain cutoff.

In this script I show the maximum and average workload over a set of snapshots:

```
select s.snap_id,
to_char(begin_interval_time, 'dd-mon-yy-
hh24:mi') BEG,
Round(maxval/100) MAX, Round(average/100) AVG
from dba_hist_snapshot s,
DBA_HIST_SYSMETRIC_SUMMARY M
where s.snap_id = m.snap_id
and s.snap_id between tbd and tbd
and s.instance_number = m.instance_number
 and metric_name like 'Database Time Per Sec%'
and Round(average/100) > 2
order by 1;
```

SNAP_ID	BEG	MAX	AVG
53388	13-mar-18-00:00	7	3
53388	13-mar-18-00:00	7	3
53389	13-mar-18-01:00	7	3
53389	13-mar-18-01:00	5	2
53390	13-mar-18-02:00	7	3
53390	13-mar-18-02:00	7	2
53391	13-mar-18-03:00	4	2
53391	13-mar-18-03:00	5	3
53392	13-mar-18-04:00	4	2

SCRIPT #19 EASY WAYS TO FIND UNDO USAGE

On one of our production systems, we occasionally need to drop and recreate a gigantic index. On one occasion, we were surprised by the undo usage, we ran out of undo space, and our job actually failed. Of course, we wondered how that much undo was really needed. Did our job really need 1/2 TB of undo?

To my pleasant surprise, I discovered that there are lots of clues to help us summarize undo usage. We can simply use one of the *Dba_Hist* tables to quantify, by time and node, the undo usage. Here's one way to do it. I've used this script on our 8-node RAC cluster. It looks for a particular window of snapshots, and displays cases where the undo usage is greater than 100k blocks:

```
Select Snap_Id, Instance_Number Node,
To_Char(Begin_Time,'Hh24:Mi') Bgn,
To_Char(End_Time,'Hh24:Mi') Endtm,
Round(Undoblks/1000000,1) Megundo,
Activeblks
From Dba_Hist_Undostat
Where Snap_Id = 52316
And Instance_Number In (3,4)
And Undoblks/1000000 > .1
Order By 1,2;
```

Rolling up the Nodes

It might be useful to see the total amount of undo, rather than the individual entries. Let's do a rollup, summarizing undo for each instance for a given range of Snap_Ids. We'll filter the query, so that we only see entries for node 3, and for those snap times with undo greater than 100k:

```
Select Snap_Id, Instance_Number Node,
Round( Sum(Undoblks/1000000),1) Megundo_Blks
From Dba_Hist_Undostat
Where Snap_Id Between 52310 And 52330
And Instance_Number In (3)
And Undoblks/1000000 > .1
Group By Snap_Id, Instance_Number
Order By 1,2,3;
```

The above summary gives us a nice, simple view of undo quantity per node at any given time.

Another Way to Check

Hey, wait! Don't we already have undo information elsewhere? Yes, it's true. The rollup we just displayed should be similar to entries in another Dba_Hist table--i.e., *Dba_Hist_Sysstat*. The relevant statistic there is called, "undo change vector size." Let's query that table and see if that matches what we have found so far:

```
Select Distinct Snap_Id, Instance_Number NODE,
ROUND(((Value - Lag(Value,1) Over(Order By
Snap_Id)))/1000000,1) MBYTES_UNDO
From DBA_HIST_SYSSTAT
Where Snap_Id Between 52315 And 52322
And Stat_Name Like 'undo change%'
And Instance_Number = 3
Order By 1;
```

SNAP_ID	NODE	MBYTES_UNDO
52316	3	8404.7
52317	3	1948.2
52318	3	165.4
52319	3	751.7
52320	3	112.2
52321	3	731.2
52322	3	706.4

This script also gives the DBA a good look at the quantity of undo; note, however, this will not exactly correspond to undo blocks. It's not simply a matter of dividing the megabytes of undo by the block size. Rather, the script above will tend to undercount the actual undo blocks needed. There's at least one reason why this is so. Even a very small amount of undo will require one undo block.

SCRIPT #20 FIND MISSING INDEXES ON FOREIGN KEYS

This still happens a lot, but there is a simple way to detect this problem. Oftentimes, it leads to a discussion of *why* there is a foreign key in the first place. Just recently, I ran this script for a new application, and found 1200 missing indexes! It suggested that the designers had been overzealous in creating referential integrity.

```
Col Owner Format A12
Col Table_Name Format A22
Col Column_Name Format A20
Col Constraint_Name Format A20

Select C1.Owner, C1.Table_Name,
C1.Constraint_Name,Column_Name
From Dba_Constraints C1, Dba_Cons_Columns C2
Where Constraint_Type = 'R'
And C1.Constraint_Name = C2.Constraint_Name
And C1.Table_Name = C2.Table_Name
And Column_Name Not In
(Select Column_Name From Dba_Ind_Columns
Where Table_Name = C1.Table_Name
And Column_Position = 1)
And C1.Owner Not Like 'SYS%';
```

In this script, I first look for constraints that are "R," which means referential integrity. Then, I look to see if there is any index that has that column in the leading position. I am not interested in proofing the data dictionary, which is why I omit the SYS% users.

SCRIPT #21 OBSERVE ROLLBACK

Every so often, I need to see what kinds of transactions are in flight. For example, suppose I have killed a job, and I want to see how quickly the rollback is progressing.

To accomplish this, I run a script that I call, "Rollback." It gives me the exact details on transactions in progress.

```
Select Start_Time,
       S.Sid, S.Username,
       S.Osuser, S.Status,
       T.Used_Ublk,
       T.Used_Urec,
       S.Machine
  From V$Transaction T,
       V$Rollname    R,
       V$Session     S
 Where T.Addr   = S.Taddr
   And T.Xidusn = R.Usn
       Order By 1;
```

You can customize the columns if you need less information. Here's a simpler version, just showing the "bare bones" information:

```
Select S.Sid,
       S.Username, S.Osuser,
       S.Status,
       T.Used_Ublk, T.Used_Urec
  From V$Transaction T,
       V$Rollname    R,
       V$Session     S
 Where T.Addr   = S.Taddr
   And T.Xidusn = R.Usn
 Order By 1;
```

SID	USERNAME	OSUSER	STATUS	USED_UBLK	USED_UREC
1535	MDADM	applABC	ACTIVE	1	1

SCRIPT #22 SIMPLE *EXPLAIN PLAN* SCRIPTS

I have a few scripts for performing Explain Plan that I have used for many years. I think every DBA has their favorite way to do this, but these scripts are simple, yet effective.

```
Select     Id, Parent_Id, Cost,
Lpad (' ', Level - 1) || Operation || ' ' ||
           Options Operation, Object_Name,
Options
From       Plan_Table
Where      Statement_Id = '&Stmt_Id'
Start With Id = 0
And        Statement_Id = '&Stmt_Id'
Connect By Prior
           Id = Parent_Id
And        Statement_Id = '&Stmt_Id'
/
```

If I need to spot "Partition Pruning," I use this script, which adds the fields, *Partition_Start* and *Partition_Stop*:

```
Select     Id, Parent_Id, Cost,
Lpad (' ', Level - 1) || Operation || ' ' ||
           Options Operation,
Partition_Start, Partition_Stop
Object_Name, Options
From       Plan_Table
Where      Statement_Id = '&Stmt_Id'
Start With Id = 0
And        Statement_Id = '&Stmt_Id'
Connect By Prior
           Id = Parent_Id
And        Statement_Id = '&Stmt_Id'
/
```

SCRIPT #23 SPOT EXCESSIVE "ACTIVE TIME" SESSIONS

Some recent column additions enable the DBA to easily spot long-running sessions. By finding the difference between Sysdate and Sql_Exec_Start, we can find the duration.

It is very common to find "orphan" sessions that were disconnected a long time ago, but yet Oracle thinks they are still "active."

I like to run the script below to list sql that has been running over 9999 seconds:

```
Select Username, S.Inst_Id Inst,Module, Sid,
S.Sql_Id,
(Sysdate-Sql_Exec_Start)*24*60*60 Secs,
Sql_Text
From Gv$Session S, Gv$Sqltext T
Where S.Sql_Id = T.Sql_Id
And S.Inst_Id = T.Inst_Id
And Piece = 0
And (Sysdate-Sql_Exec_Start)*24*60*60 > 9999
--Look For 99 Seconds
Order By 2,3;
```

I use a cut-off of 9999 seconds; of course, you can set your own limits. You may also want to filter-out any jobs that are expected to run a long time.

OPTIMIZATION TECHNIQUES

Once the problem is spotted, you will have to figure out how to deal with it. This is a huge area, but there are certain techniques that I have found useful.

Didn't Follow my Recommendations

Different DBAs will use different methods, of course, but you would be wise to consider the tactics listed in this section.

TECH #1 DIVIDE THE PROBLEM INTO PIECES

Closely related to "Simplifying" is *Breaking the Problem into Pieces*. Actually this approach is really just another form of simplifying. The principle is the same—we want to try to remove distractions and irrelevant information, so that what remains is the *essence* of the problem.

Most SQL statement difficulties are due to a very few causes—very often, only *one*. It is very common for the performance expert to make just one change, and see remarkable performance changes!

Of course, having just one core issue to solve cannot be guaranteed for every case, but this observation should be encouraging news to Oracle professionals—especially those interested in SQL tuning.

The "divide" approach to simplifying performance problems would not be so helpful if individual parts of SQL code tended to contribute equally to the bottleneck. Generally speaking, however, the parts of the SQL code do *not* contribute equally. If ten tables are being joined, the problem will *not* be 10% degradation related to each table; more likely, the problem will be 80% due to one table, and 20% due to one other table.

Break up SQL Code

The "Break into Pieces" approach is especially useful when tackling complicated SQL code. Oftentimes, what begins as a very complex SQL problem can be divided into several parts, each of which is much more manageable.

To illustrate this approach, consider the following SQL statement. This code retrieves a list of employees from three separate tables, meeting three separate conditions:

```
Select Emp_name from Emp
Where Zip_Code like '92%'
Union
Select Emp_name from Term_Employees
Where Term_Date < Sysdate - 365
Union
Select Emp_name from Managers
Where dept_id = 1000;
```

If this SQL statement were to have a performance problem, the separation tactic would be very obvious—simply divide the SQL before each *UNION* statement. Then, attention could be individually directed at each of the three SQL statements. Each statement could be checked for good run time. Of course, most SQL statements will not be so trivial; nevertheless, the concept will be the same.

Consider this slightly more complicated example

```
Select Emp_name from Emp
Where Dept_id in
   (Select Dept_id from Dept
    Where Dept_Name like 'ENGINEER%');
```

This SQL statement can easily be divided into an *outer* query and an *inner* query. The inner query runs first, then it feeds the rows into the outer query. Naturally, both pieces must run efficiently if the entire statement is to run well.

First, then, we must determine which of the two parts is the problem. Is it the outer query, or the inner query? Let's separate them, and find out.

First, list the inner query:

```
Select Dept_id from Dept
Where Dept_Name like 'ENGINEER%';
```

Then, the outer query could be modeled as:

```
Select Emp_name from Emp
Where Dept_id = 'N'
```

Now that the SQL is broken into its parts, simple timing tests will easily show which piece is the culprit. To check the timing of the outer query, one simple approach would be to simply substitute a typical value for 'N' and check the performance for this one small SQL statement in Sql*Plus.

TECH #2 USE "SUPER INDEXES"

Besides looking at how well an index satisfies the *where* clause, it's useful to see if an index can also satisfy the *Select* clause! This performance tactic requires that we build an index such that the table listed in the SQL is *never accessed*. This means that every single field in the *Select* clause is *fully satisfied* via the index.

This benefit might seem to be minor, but this trick has proven its worth time and time again. It is most beneficial when trying to eke out the last little bit of performance improvement. For instance, this tactic may be useful for some table joins, when it is a "close call" between choosing a nested loop join or one of the other join methods. The super index can make the nested loop option achieve much better performance than otherwise. With the new super index, many *table* accesses can be eliminated, even though there might still be a large number of index accesses. This can sometimes make a huge difference in run time.

The optimizer may detect the existence of this "super" index on its own; in some cases, however, it will be necessary to use the Sql hint *INDEX* to persuade the optimizer to use the proper index. To use the hint INDEX, simply insert the table name (or alias, if applicable), plus the index name.

The syntax for the INDEX hint is:

```
Select /*+Index(Table Indexname) */
```

Note that the second argument, *Indexname*, is optional. If more than one index is provided, the index with the "cheapest" cost will be used. If no indexes are listed, the optimizer will once again choose the index that appears to provide the lowest cost.

TECH #3 REDUCE RESULT SET AS *MUCH* AS POSSIBLE, AS *EARLY* AS POSSIBLE.

An important way to speed-up joins is by reducing or "winnowing" the result set as early in the join process as possible. In joins, this means applying restrictive conditions as early in the process as possible. The goal is to achieve the *largest percentage reduction* as possible. Note that this is *not* the same as beginning with the smallest table.

The analyst should concentrate on reducing the result set *proportionately*, not simply using the smallest table as the first table in the join. A percentage reduction in the first few tables generally means that a similar reduction will accrue in the subsequent tables.

Let's consider an analogy to show why it is so critical to reduce the result set early in the process. Suppose a citizen of a small town goes to the county "Office of Vital Statistics." He asks the clerk for all birth certificates for the year 1989. The clerk says, "*All* the records--are you sure?"

The requestor responds, "Certainly. Please give me *all* the birth certificates." The clerk shuffles from one file cabinet to another, and finally carts up all birth certificates for the specified year. The citizen looks them over then says, "Now which ones are for people whose last name starts with 'Z'? I really only want those."

The clerk loads up all the boxes again, leaving the citizen with just one small folder. The requestor finds the birth certificate of interest, jots down the desired information, and then walks out, leaving the fuming clerk behind.

Performing tuning with the Oracle engine works much the same way. It is always best to reduce the request as much as possible, as soon as possible.

TECH #4 UNDERSTAND STRENGTH/WEAKNESS OF NESTED LOOP JOINS

This method works especially well for queries that are very selective, and only return a small result set. Consider the following query, and see how Oracle would satisfy this query using a nested loop join.

```
Select Cust_Id, Address, Phone, Plan
From Customers C, LD_Plan P
Where C.Cust_Id = P.Cust_Id
And Customer_Name = 'BOB JOHNSON';
```

1) Oracle starts with one table (called the *driving* table) and find all rows that match the criteria in the *where* clause.

2) Using this result set from table one, Oracle uses an index on the second table to find entries that match the value of the join field. (Find all rows in the *LD_Plan* table that have Cust_Id = 1001.)

3) Using the row identifiers in the index on the LD_PLAN table, retrieve the matching rows from the second table.

4) Return the information from both tables for all matching rows.

For a nested loop join, the second table (the *driven* table) should have an index on the join column. In our example, this means that the *LD_Plan* table must be indexed on the Cust_Id column.

Performance of nested loop joins

There are a few other interesting aspects of nested loop joins. One interesting benefit is that nested loop joins return the *first rows* faster than the other join methods. This happens because with the nested loop there is no need to wait until the "end." The nested loop join provides the final result "a little at a time."

A secondary advantage of nested loop joins is that a nested loop join does not require *sorting*. The result set from the driving table is simply used as input—to *drive*--the second table. (As we will see, the *sorting* operation is a key factor in the sort-merge join, and can make it a poor option.)

A third benefit of the nested loop join is that this join method can be used whether or not the join criteria is an *equi*-join (e.g., uses the '=' symbol for the join condition.) In contrast, both the sort-merge and hash join methods are only applicable for equi-joins.

Limitations of Nested Loop Joins

The above example works well using the nested loop methodology; however, this was a special case. In the following SQL, the query has been modified to find the same information, but for those customers whose first name is John.

```
SELECT Cust_Name, Phone, DVD_Name,
From Customer C, Rented R
 WHERE C.Cust_Id = R.Cust_Id
    AND Cust_Name like 'John%';
```

This query is clearly *not* suitable for a nested loop because the result set from the first table will be very large. If a nested loop join were used, the optimizer would have to make *thousands* of index lookups for the second table; this would be followed by thousands of table lookups to get the *DVD_Name* column. Not only is a nested loop join a bad idea in this new case—it is probably the *worst possible choice* for queries such as this.

TECH #5 USE MATERIALIZED VIEW FOR REPEATED REPORTS

Materialized views are objects equivalent to what was formerly called *snapshots*. A bit of trivia: Many of the concepts and procedures that were used with snapshots are equally applicable to materialized views.

Like its name suggests, a materialized view *really contains the rows* that are defined by the Sql provided during its definition. This means that storage space is consumed, similar to the space consumed by a table or index. So when a materialized view is created, tablespace name and storage parameters are specified, in the same manner as for a table.

A materialized view is thus very different from a "normal" (non-materialized) view. A "normal" view is actually only an equation residing in the data dictionary. A normal view consumes no storage space because the rows are dynamically fetched when the view is queried. In contrast, a materialized view consumes space because the rows are *materialized*.

Why use a MV?

Although a materialized view can be used in conjunction with any application, the feature is most useful in *data warehouse* applications. In order to see why this is so, we must briefly describe some features of a large data warehouse and explore some typical performance problems.

In a large data warehouse application, the volume of data often makes it unwise to repeatedly perform complex Sql queries that must process millions of rows. For instance, a typical report for a large corporation might tabulate the total sales, sorted by region, for all product lines. This type of report might take 30 minutes to run *each time it is requested*.

These long wait times associated with reports are often considered unacceptable. As a way to reduce this run time, the database architect often builds tables that hold *aggregate*, or pre-joined data. These pre-built tables are typically called "summary tables." With these new summary tables, the reports can run much faster. Instead of performing the time-consuming joins and fetches, the report will simply query the *summary* tables instead.

Materialized views provide some unique advantages, and are a good option to use in place of summary tables. For instance, if the summary data were housed in a regular table, it would need to be truncated or rebuilt every time the database was updated. Materialized views, on the other hand, have several "refresh" options that simplify and expedite the repopulation of the summary data. Additionally, materialized views allow the use of "query rewrite," an important performance improvement measure, discussed later in this chapter.

TECH #6 UNDERSTAND MV REFRESH OPTIONS

When first creating a materialized view, it is possible to either immediately populate the object, or to do it later, via a call to a 'refresh' procedure. The two options are called *Build Immediate* and *Build Deferred*. For example, the following script creates an *unpopulated* materialized view of *Sales*, grouped by *Employee*:

```
Create Materialized View Emp_Sales_Summary
Build Deferred As
Select Employee_Name,
Sum (Sales_Amt) Sales_Total
From Sales
Group By Employee_Name;
```

Note that the above view will remain unpopulated until a refresh is commanded.

Refresh options

Besides deciding whether to immediately populate a materialized view, there are several more refresh options to consider. When a materialized view is first created, one of two *refresh execution modes* is specified: either *On Demand* or *On Commit*. In most cases (and especially for data warehouse projects), it is appropriate to use the *On Demand* option.

The On Demand option is often used because the oracle engine only performs the work to refresh the view at *set times*, rather than upon every committed transaction on an underlying table. Thus, for a data warehouse application, a refresh of all materialized views is typically commanded when the nightly load has completed.

Another option to consider is the *refresh method*. This option specifies what should happen when a refresh occurs—should Oracle try to *completely* refresh the materialized view, or should it only try to find the changed rows? There are four refresh methods that may be specified: *Complete, Fast, Force,* or *Never.*

Just like it sounds, a *complete* refresh will perform a truncate of the view, followed by a complete repopulation. This could be a good choice if the underlying tables have been extensively changed.

The Fast refresh, on the other hand, performs an *incremental* update—that is, only *changed* rows are added to the materialized view. For very large databases, the *Fast* refresh offers obvious performance advantages, especially in the case where only a small portion of the underlying tables have been changed. Although this option is slightly more complicated to setup, the performance gains are usually worth the effort.

The *Force* option means that a *fast refresh* will be used if possible; otherwise a complete refresh will be performed. Finally, the *Never* option means that the materialized view will never be refreshed.

At first glance, these refresh options may appear confusing. So let's turn to an example that illustrates the refresh options discussed above. The following script creates a materialized view that will be updated with a fast refresh, but only upon demand.

```
Create Materialized View Emp_Sales_Summary
Build Immediate
Refresh Fast On Demand As
Select Employee_Name,
Sum (Sales_Amt) Sales_Total
From Sales
Group By Employee_Name;
```

TECH #7 "DIVIDE AND CONQUER" TABLE JOINS

A more sophisticated use of the "Break into pieces" approach can be applied to table joins. Simplification of table joins is important, because of the frequency of this form of SQL. It is very common to have SQL statements with a variety of table joins, in which only one or two of the tables joined are causing the performance problem.

In complicated SQL queries with table joins, one useful tactic is to *remove* a few of the tables in the join in order to simplify the join, and thereby distinguish which tables are really "performance drivers" for the SQL in question. In other words, we try to find out which tables are on the "critical path"—which ones are really the performance "drivers."

Let's consider a simple query with five tables involved in joins. For this example, we are not concerned with the exact method of joining; any of the join methods--Nested Loop, Hash Join, or Sort/Merge--can be assumed for this example.

Let us assume that they are listed in the join order, left to right. So, Table_A is the driving table in the first join, and Table_B is the *driven* table. The result from the first join then becomes the driver for the second join, etc.

The SQL used for this query is:

```
Select A. Emp_id
From
Table_A A,
Table_B B
Table_C C,
Table_D D,
Table_E E
Where
     A. Deptno = B.deptno
And B.Site = C.Site
And C.Division = D.Division
And D.Office = E.Office;
```

Assuming that there is a performance problem with this query, we are faced with the question, "Which join or which table is causing the bottleneck?"

One good way to answer that question is to *systematically divide the SQL statement*, thus greatly simplifying the root cause analysis. By splitting the SQL into pieces, the core of the performance problem can be quickly determined.

There are several good ways to start. One idea that immediately comes to mind is eliminating Table_D and Table_E from the SQL entirely. This would then leave us with the very simple join

Notice that we have roughly divided the SQL statement in half. The next step would be to run the simplified SQL that refers to only Table_A through Table_C, and check performance. The objective would be to see if the Problem stays with Table_A through Table_C, or whether the problem has disappeared.

Keep the Same Join Method

When simplifying table join code as a method of understanding a more complex expression, it is important that the simplified SQL retain the same join order and join method as the original. Otherwise, we are not "comparing apples to apples," and our analysis will be misleading.

Thus, in our example, we should verify that the simplified SQL has an execution plan that joins the tables in order Table_A, Table_B, Table_C.

Suppose that our simplified query with just a few joins still runs poorly. Since there are only three tables (and two joins) involved, the troubleshooting process has been greatly simplified. There are not too many choices left to investigate.

On the other hand, if the simplified query runs well, the next logical step would be to "add back" Table_D, then Table_E, and determine at which point the performance problem returns.

TECH #8 TABLE SCANS ARE NOT ALWAYS BAD

Indexes are not always the best choices. In fact, some of the *worst possible* execution plans use indexes! This fact is something that many junior analysts often fail to appreciate. Many times, frustrated developers have approached the DBA and exclaimed, "I don't know what's wrong—the query is using an index!" Although indexes *generally* assist the Oracle engine, they are not correct in *all* cases.

In situations where a full table scan is appropriate, the alternative of index scan (followed by table access) can often produce amazingly bad performance. Indexes are often a good choice, but sometimes are a poor option compared to a full table scan. In cases where most of the table needs to be accessed anyway, indexes are usually an inappropriate alternative.

Table Scans not always Bad

Full table (or partition) scans are often appropriate. Especially with the improvements made in disk access time, disk caching, and multi-block reads, a full table scan is often an excellent alternative.

It's true that indexes are *generally* a good idea because response time is *generally* better, and resource consumption is *generally* less when indexes are used. Thus, for queries that impose a severe limiting condition—e.g., Employee_Id = '12345', an index is almost certainly the best option. There is no question that queries such as this should be using an index.

As the restrictive condition "loosens," however, the choice between index and full table scan will become less obvious. At some point, the cost of the full table scan will be less than numerous index and table lookups.

Resource consumption and run time for each of the alternatives can easily be checked in SQL*Plus. (SQL*Plus *Autotrace* is an excellent way to get a quick measurement of resource consumption.) Just remember that a full table scan does not mean that the optimizer is making an error; it could be the correct choice for a particular SQL statement.

TECH #9 UNDERSTAND HOW WAIT EVENTS WORK

In each Oracle database, each process is either actively *doing* something, or *waiting* for something to happen. The whole philosophy in the wait method of performance analysis is to determine what Oracle is waiting for, and decide if any of the detected Wait Events can be eliminated.

Here are some ideas of what the database engine could be waiting for. Any one of these could potentially lead to a performance bottleneck:

- Writing to disk
- Reading from disk single-block
- Reading from disk multi-block
- Sql*net traffic to and from the client
- Writing to the control file
- Reading from the control file
- Writing to the redo log file
- Locks and latches
- Waiting for space in the log buffer

Unfortunately, the analyst cannot simply focus on the "worst" Wait Events, because many Wait Events are "normal." Over the course of a day, it is normal for the database engine to wait many times, for a variety of reasons. Most of these "waits" are expected, and neither the DBA nor the end users will even be aware of these miniscule delays.

For example, it is very common for the database to wait for a user to supply input. This situation is especially true for OLTP (Online Transaction Processing) applications. While the database is "waiting" on the user, a certain Wait event will accrue wait time. Oracle calls this particular event "Sql*Net message from client." Naturally, large values for this Wait event do *not* indicate a performance problem, but merely a normal state of operation.

Normal and Abnormal Wait Events

The trick then is to find out which of the Wait Events are *not* normal. This is a bit of a challenge, since many of the largest wait times that are detected will actually be irrelevant, or pertain to options that are not being used. Some experience with the Wait views will be needed before the analyst begins to get a "feel" for which information is critical, and which Wait events on his particular system can safely be disregarded. Wait events will clearly depend on the exact application that is being used, so for each database, the normal wait events might be a little different.

On the other hand, certain events are very important, and should generally not be disregarded. These events indicate preventable performance delays; thus, these events will prove useful to the Oracle Detective as he investigates performance bottlenecks.

Wait Events are a Good *Starting Point*

The Wait views indicate what activity is holding up the processing, but they don't show *why*. That is, the Wait views are not really an "end point," but a good *starting point*. Once some "clues" are identified, the analyst will usually need to look at other areas to help identify the underlying cause of the delay.

For instance, if the Wait views indicate that the Oracle engine is waiting for disk I/O, the analyst will probably want to find out which SQL statement is responsible for that activity. Thus, he will probably decide to query the V$Sql view, which will show the exact Sql that has being run. In fact, querying the V$Sql view will be a subsequent step in many cases. Just as the Wait event indicates the area of delay, the V$Sql view identifies the actual SQL statement that is responsible for the delay.

TECH #10 REMOVE THE NETWORK EFFECT

For SQL queries that return a large data set, it will be necessary to distinguish between delays due to network transfer time, and delays due to actual database processing. The Oracle analyst could easily spend hours troubleshooting a SQL problem that is no problem at all.

For instance, suppose that a developer reports a problem with a certain function in the application. The application appears to be delayed 30 seconds every time this function is run. Upon investigation, the Oracle analyst discovers that the SQL returns 10,000 rows. The question then is, is the database responsible for the 30-second delay, or is the network transfer time really the culprit?

In order to "assign the blame," the analyst must somehow remove the network effects, so that the database contribution alone can be determined. One simple method is to change the SQL so the optimizer has to perform the same work, but the final result set is really only a *summary*—not the actual rows.

For instance, the analyst can ask the Oracle engine to only supply the *maximum values* of the result set, or change the SQL to send the result set to a temporary table. In both cases, the network effect has been removed, so that whatever delays remains must be due solely to the database. (If you do change the query, just make sure that you don't accidentally change the execution plan.)

TECH #11 REMOVE EFFECT OF DISPLAYING DATA

When testing queries in Sql*Plus to check runtime, the runtime reported by SQL*Plus will be greatly distorted when a large number of rows are included in the result set. One good idea is to temporarily remove any influence due to the time spent displaying the results. Then, the measured runtime must be due to just the database—not the display time. This is especially important when testing queries that return more than just a few rows.

As with the previous tip, it is usually simple to slightly modify the SQL to achieve the same execution plan, but without the entire result set. For instance, simply change the SQL to use the MAX function, or some similar modification that will require the Oracle engine to perform essentially the same work.

Take care to ensure that the optimizer must still process the same information as in the original SQL statement; otherwise, the modified SQL may not accurately reflect the work required.

TECH #12 DON'T IGNORE LOGICAL READS

Since physical I/O is more expensive than logical I/O, the Oracle analyst might be tempted to ignore logical I/O. This would be a big mistake; looking at excessing logical reads, or "buffer gets" is often a great way to tune a query.

By solving logical reads, the physical reads will be solved as a necessary side effect. If logical reads are substantially reduced, the physical reads will normally be reduced in a similar proportion. (After all, how can you have physical reads without logical reads first?)

The reverse is not true however. Changing the execution plan to reduce physical reads does not necessarily reduce logical reads—in fact, if the execution plan is drastically changed so that physical reads are eliminated, logical reads may be much higher, and lead to a much worse response time!

For instance, index blocks are often read from cache, but blocks from tables are much less likely to already be in cache. So, a query that requires many index reads will lead to a large number of logical reads, but few physical reads. This may or may not be a good idea, but it will make the number of physical reads look "good." Some execution plans will thus avoid physical reads at the cost of a massive number of index lookups—which is typically not a good tradeoff.

A further reason to focus on logical reads is that logical reads can often lead to massive CPU consumption. For instance, consider two tables that are joined in a nested loop. Normally, a nested loop is a good choice when the result set from the driving table (i.e., the *first* table) is fairly small. The Oracle engine loops through the first table, then uses the small result set to check an index in the second table for the corresponding entries that satisfy the join condition. With a small result set from the first table, the subsequent work is small—perhaps just a few index look-ups.

But what if the result set is *not* small? In that case, the engine must loop through every row of the large result set, processing each row one by one. The response time could easily be an order of magnitude worse—even though very little physical I/O is occurring!

TECH #13 USE SET OPERATIONS FOR BIG DATA

This is a very powerful method, which many DBAs do not know how to use. Set operations include operations like these:

- **MINUS**
- **INTERSECT**
- **UNION**
- **UNION ALL**

These are commonly used when the result set requires manipulating large groups of data. For example, if you needed to find the rows that satisfy one query, but are *not* included in another, you could use the MINUS operation. For large result sets, this is often a better choice than the *not in* syntax.

Other examples would be finding the *common* rows using INTERSECT, or finding the rows in *either* query using UNION or UNION ALL.

Note that UNION differs from UNION ALL in that the duplicates are removed in the former operation.

It takes just a few minutes to convert your sql to set operations. If you are dealing with millions of rows, for example, it is a wise choice.

TECH #14 KNOW THE DIFFERENCE: *SEQUENTIAL* VERSUS *SCATTERED* READS

- A sequential read is a *single-block* read.

- A scattered read is a *multi-block* read. On recent databases, this is often called *direct* read.

OLTP systems typically have large amounts of sequential reads, since most queries use efficient indexes, and just retrieve a few blocks of data for each query. Batch jobs will often perform direct reads, since full table scans are much more common.

Naturally, it is critical that you understand what type of disk problem you are facing before you create a solution.

TECH #15 TABLE PARTITIONING CAN *HURT* PERFORMANCE

Depending on the exact queries that are executed, it is very possible that queries on partitioned tables will run worse than a non-partitioned table. Although people are often surprised by this result, it is not at all unusual. In fact, one of the main tasks when partitioning tables is to ensure against this possibility.

The key point is this: Is the partitioning key contained in the *where* clause? If not, the optimizer will not be able to restrict the scope of work to just a few partitions. That is, *partition pruning* will not occur.

Depending on the type of indexes (local versus global), this can have a terrible performance impact. Consider a very large table, Emp_*History*, which has been partitioned into 52 weekly partitions (based on employee start date.). Now look at the query below:

```
Select *
from Emp_History
where Dept = 101;
```

In the above query, Oracle can use a local index on *Dept*. However, the *where* clause does not include the partition key. So, if the local index on Dept is used, Oracle has no choice but to scan *all 52 partitions*. Without partitioning, the same query would have resulted in only 1 index range scan.

TECH #16 FIX PROBLEM WITH "BITMAP CONVERSION FROM ROWIDS"

Admittedly, this is an odd problem. In recent Oracle versions, the optimizer sometimes makes a terrible mistake, opting for a tricky move called "bitmap conversion from rowids." This often results in terrible performance—sometimes 100x worse than otherwise! (The optimizer appears to badly misjudge the cost of using a non-selective index.)

You can turn off this feature at the database level (in the init.ora file), or alter any session that encounters the problem, like this:

```
Alter Session Set "_b_tree_bitmap_plans" = False;
```

When the optimizer selects the execution path, the typical execution plan will look like this:

```
SELECT STATEMENT
  SORT GROUP BY
   TABLE ACCESS BY INDEX ROWID
USER_LIST_TABLE
    NESTED LOOPS
     TABLE ACCESS FULL                USERS
     BITMAP CONVERSION TO ROWIDS
      BITMAP AND
       BITMAP CONVERSION FROM ROWIDS
        INDEX RANGE SCAN              TAB1_PK
       BITMAP CONVERSION FROM ROWIDS
        INDEX RANGE SCAN              TAB2_FK
```

TECH #17 *SKIP-SCAN* IS OFTEN BAD

Skip scan refers to an optimizer feature, whereby a composite index is used to resolve a query even if the column of interest is not the leading column of the index. Oracle is able to *skip* to the desired column in the index.

To accomplish skip scan, Oracle performs a separate scan for each distinct value in the prefixed index column. That is, Oracle resolves the query as if the sql had a series of values in the *where* clause—each of which calls for an index scan. Given the nature of how it works, skip scan may be a good choice, but will not be the right choice for many situations. In many cases, it will not be the best choice.

In the execution plan, a skip scan step will be noted as

```
INDEX SKIP SCAN
```

Of course, having the appropriate index, with the matching columns in the prefix, is generally best, but there may be reasons that a new index is not feasible, or perhaps the performance from skip scan proves to be good enough.

TECH #18 DIAGRAM COMPLICATED JOINS

I first learned about diagramming complicated sql from a white paper by Daniel Tow, about 20 years ago. His white paper was one of the most important papers I've read. (Daniel now runs the "singingsql" site.)

The idea is, make a diagram showing the join connections, and note the approximate size of tables. Also note, below each table, major filtering conditions. Of course, these are tables you want to join early. As shown below, the diagram will look a lot like an "E-R Diagram."

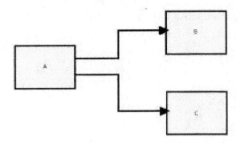

Once you create this simple diagram, you can decide the join order, based on using the most restrictive filtering conditions as early as possible. You can also see which indexes will be required. If you have one object in the diagram connected to *nothing*--you've just found a Cartesian product!

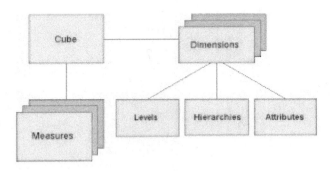

TECH #19 SEVEN THINGS TO CHECK IN AWR REPORTS

Sometimes we just want to get a quick idea of how things look on a database. Reviewing an AWR report is one way to do that.

CHECK THE TOP-5 FOREGROUND EVENTS

Almost always, a database will be waiting most often on disk reads-- usually sequential reads for OLTP-type applications, or direct path read (or scattered read) for databases running batch jobs doing full scans. Very often, CPU time is the next event.

CHECK THE SEQUENTIAL READ RATE

The sequential read rate is a great metric. Disk latency should always be below 10 ms, or at least 100 reads/sec. Depending on how the SAN is caching data, the sequential read rate is sometimes as low as 2 ms.

REVIEW TOP-SQL BY ELAPSED TIME

This is a convenient, easy way to see the longest runtime for that period.

CHECK FOR EXTREME DISK CONSUMERS

It's a good idea to know which sql is doing all the disk reads.

CHECK FOR LOGICAL READS HOGS

This is really helpful to spot inefficient sql, because sub-optimum sql often uses a ton of gets per execution.

SPOT UNUSUAL SYSTEM LOAD

I like to look at the change in load by time, as shown in the OS Detail. If there is any problem with log syncs, or slowness performing a ton of transactions, it's worth seeing how often the user is committing. You can see this under the section, "Instance Activity,"

CHECK TOP CONSUMERS OF READS

This is useful to see if there are any objects that are very "hot."

TECH #20 BECOME AN EXPERT AT ACTIVE SESSION HISTORY

I've noticed that many DBAs are only vaguely aware of the capability of Active Session History, or *ASH*. This is a mistake, because ASH is one of the most powerful diagnostic tools we have.

I often describe ASH as a "Poor Man's Tracing" tool. With just a simple script, you can see what a session was doing recently--or even days prior. Of course, ASH only shows sessions that are indeed waiting, but in most cases that's exactly what you want.

Here are just a few uses:

- Listing the top sql for a long report
- Tracking down a blocking session, and the object blocked
- Determining what type of disk reads are holding things up
- Finding the Sql causing frequent redo log sync (commits)

Of course, there are dozens more uses. I find it most helpful to develop my own script, instead of running the canned "ASH Report." I have two main types of ASH scripts For recent events, I use the *V$* version; for prior events, use the *DBA_HIST* version

V$ Version

For checking recent events (that will likely still be in the shared pool):

```
with p1 as (select /*+parallel(a 8) */
distinct * from gv$active_session_history A
where wait_time = 0
and sql_id is not null
and sample_time like '06-FEB-18%AM'
) select substr(sample_time,1,14) tt, module,
sql_id, sql_exec_id, count(*) from p1
group by substr(sample_time,1,14), module,
sql_id, sql_exec_id
having count(*) > 10;
order by 1;
```

The field *Sql_Exec_Id* is a really special field; it shows you the exact execution number of a particular sql. In other words, if it's the same number, it's the same execution of that sql_id.

DBA_Hist Version

Here's an example for ASH going back in time a little:

```
with p1 as (select /*+parallel(a 8) */
distinct *
from dba_hist_active_sess_history A
where snap_id between 1152 and 1157
and wait_time = 0
and sql_id = 'cnxsz5na01r4s'
) select sql_id, sql_exec_id, module, count(*)
from p1
group by sql_id, sql_exec_id, module
having count(*) > 5;
```

There are tons of variations you can build. For instance, I often join to the *Dba_Objects* view to show the Object_Name.

TECH #21 WATCH PARALLELISM ACTUALLY ACHIEVED

On busy systems that employ lots of parallel processing, it sometimes happens that a job does not "get" the parallelism it has requested. This can lead to bewildering delays—especially since the PHV (Plan Hash Value) stays the same, regardless of the parallelism achieved.

The easiest way to spot this problem is to review the historical stats for the sql in question. The parallelism is found by looking at "PX_Servers." Here is a good way to review this:

```
Select Snap_Id, Instance_Number,
Plan_Hash_Value,
Px_Servers_Execs_Delta PX ,
Executions_Delta, Rows_Processed_Delta,
Round(Elapsed_Time_Delta/1000000/60) Mins,
Round(Disk_Reads_Delta) Disk
From Dba_Hist_Sqlstat S
Where Sql_Id = 'tbd'
Order By 1;
```

Sometimes the PX field is difficult to interpret, as the optimizer will count the parallelism differently, depending on the exact sql. Also, the parallelism count will typically be noted only during the Snapshot_Id when the sql actually completed. Nevertheless, by looking for changes in the parallelism achieved, you can spot a problem.

In the result set below, you can see how the parallelism went from 50 to 12 in a later run.

SNAP_ID	INSTANCE_NUMBER	PLAN_HASH_VALUE	PX
1202	1	759237987	50
1202	2	759237987	0
1203	1	759237987	0
1204	1	759237987	0
1205	1	759237987	0
1206	1	759237987	0
1207	1	759237987	0
1208	1	759237987	12

CHANGING EXECUTION PLANS

This section contains some valuable tips on how to change execution plans (or keep them from changing!) There are some very tricky things to understand.

EXEC #1 UNDERSTAND COST OF SQL PLAN MANAGEMENT (SPM)

The strength of SPM is that it stops executions plans from changing. However, there are many occasions where the DBA wants *lots* of execution plans. In these situations, SPM can be a real hindrance.

Here are some cases where the plans would be expected to change:

- Database parameter change
- Statistics update
- Index changes

The stated goal is very broad-scoped, suggesting that it will help performance to never degrade due to changed execution plans. Here's the problem: If you try to control 100% of all sql, the whole thing becomes very cumbersome. So, the question is, how can we DBAs most easily adapt SPM so that it allows plans to change when we want them to change?

Option 1: Start SPM Afresh

This strikes me as a poor choice. It is unlikely that one can simply "start over" with SPM--that is, remove all baselines, and start with new plans. The reason is, we likely have certain troublesome Sql for which SPM is keeping the plan constant. For these, we do not want the plan to change--we want the plan to stay exactly the way it is.

Option 2: Mark Special Sql

One option is to mark the special Sql (perhaps a special name), so that we remove all the other baselines but not the special ones. This method would make SPM imitate Stored Outlines, by creating a special class of Sql. In this approach, the burden is on the DBA to make sure the special baselines are never removed. To ensure that, all the baselines would have to be backed up at some point. This strikes me as a very risky strategy.

Option 3: Manually Select Sql

SPM provides the option of "evolving" plan baselines to include other plans. To make the evolving process simpler, one option is to gather baselines only for a limited set of sql--for certain key functions or jobs.

That way, there aren't as many sql that will change when new indexes are added.

Option 4: Use SPM on Small Set

I believe this is what most DBAs are doing. It appears that most users are only using SPM on a small number of sql. In this scenario, there really isn't much of a problem in the development/test environment, since there are so few sql involved.

Using SPM in this way seems to work fine; however, it's not at all how the SPM designers envisioned it working. Using it with just a small set of sql is using it *just like stored outlines,* except more complicated.

Handling Plan Changes in the Test Environment

Assuming that "Option 4" is being used, we only have a limited set of baseline plans to manage—so this won't be too bad. Here is how it can work:

- Introduce the change (new index, etc.)
- Run the various programs that trigger key sql.
- Identify the sql that "want" to change (i.e., have a just-created baseline, but not yet accepted)
- Drop or disable all baselines for those sql.
- Re-run the programs and confirm performance is acceptable.

When ready to go to production, the only needed step is to run the script to disable the baselines for the sql that we want to change plans.

EXEC #2 HOW TO DROP A SQL PLAN BASELINE

If you have added some indexes, or made other changes, you may need to drop some SPM baselines. Here's a simple way to accomplish that.

First find the plan in question

We first need to find the "sql_handle." In the example below, I am looking for a sql that performs an update.

```
select sql_handle,
enabled,accepted,fixed ,
round(elapsed_time/1000000/60) mins,executions
execs,
substr( module,1,12) module,
substr(sql_text,1,40) sqltext
from dba_sql_plan_baselines
where elapsed_time > 9400000000
AND UPPER(SQL_TEXT) LIKE 'UPDATE%'
AND EXECUTIONS > 33
order by elapsed_time desc;
```

Now, Drop the Baseline

```
declare
  v_dropped_plans number;
BEGIN
  v_dropped_plans :=
DBMS_SPM.DROP_SQL_PLAN_BASELINE (
    sql_handle => 'TBD');
  DBMS_OUTPUT.PUT_LINE('dropped ' ||
v_dropped_plans || ' plans');
END;
/
```

EXEC #3 LIST YOUR SPM BASELINES

Here's a simple way to see what kind of outlines you currently have. You might wonder if your database has ANY outlines, or you just might want to find poorly-running sql that already has a SPM baseline.

```
set linesize 200
col mins format 999999
col Module format a12
col sqltext format a40
col sql_handle format a22

select sql_handle,
enabled,accepted,fixed ,
round(elapsed_time/1000000/60) mins,executions
execs,
substr( module,1,12) module,
substr(sql_text,1,40) sqltext
from dba_sql_plan_baselines
where elapsed_time > 99900000000
order by elapsed_time desc;
```

In the script above, I only want to see the baselines for long-running sql. Of course, you can change the filters to suit your own needs.

EXEC #4 ADD SQL HINTS USING A STORED OUTLINE

Stored outlines are an easy way to preserve a desired execution plan. This may be done for testing purposes, or to create plan stability in production environments. Oracle accomplishes the desired plan by storing a set of sql hints, which are then applied when it recognizes the sql.

For instance, suppose you are testing a particular sql statement that is causing performance difficulties. In order to perform testing, you wish to have the execution plan on your test database match the plan that is actually run on production. To accomplish this, you capture the specific sql on the database that has the desired plan. Then, you export a few outline tables. Finally, you import these tables into the target database. Now, whenever Oracle sees the sql, it will automatically apply the sql hints that guide the optimizer to the original execution plan.

What is a Stored Outline?

A stored outline *preserves* an execution plan. It's most often used in testing. Here's how it works:

1. You turn-on *outline capture*.
2. You run the sql in question.
3. Oracle watches how the sql runs & figures out what sql hints ensure the present exec plan.
4. When that *exact sql* is run in the future, Oracle applies those sql hints to keep *same* exec plan.
5. The hints are stored in 3 outline tables.

But I Want a Different Execution Plan!

What if you want a *different* exec plan to happen when you run a certain sql? How can Oracle do this, because Stored Outlines preserve an *existing* execution plan?

Here's our scheme: First, use sql hint to create the exec plan you would like to occur. (Of course, this might be a fair amount of work.) Then, trick Oracle to use the new exec plan even when we *don't* supply the sql hint.

The steps are:

- Turn on stored outline gathering.

- Run the sql on interest. Then run a second sql with *hint added*.

- We now have 2 stored outlines:
  No hint   >> Oracle uses Outline 1 (bad plan)
  With hint >> Oracle uses Outline 2 (good plan)

- *Reverse hints* so that Oracle will apply Outline 2 when it sees the sql *without* the hint. We do this by updating the hints table, *Outln.Ol$hints.*

A Tested Template

Here's the template I always use. I have used this nearly a *hundred* times to fix production problems:

```
Alter Session Set Current_Schema = [Schema Of
Intest];

CREATE OUTLINE SQLTBD FOR CATEGORY CCBTUNE ON
{SQL WITH HINT}

CREATE OUTLINE SQLTBD_FIX FOR CATEGORY CCBTUNE
ON
{REGULAR SQL}

--NOW SWITCH hints
update outln.ol$hints set ol_name =
decode(ol_name,   'SQLTBD_FIX', 'SQLTBD',
'SQLTBD', 'SQLTBD_FIX')
where ol_name in ('SQLTBD', 'SQLTBD_FIX');

drop outline SQLTBD;
```

Note that the sql text must match the exact sql of interest. You can get away with some extra spaces, but that's it. I use the AWR/Sql report to get the precise sql. (That's the AWR type of report where you give it the sql_id, not the general type of AWR report.) You don't have to do it that way, but one wrong character, and the outline won't work.

EXEC #5 WATCH FOR SECRET PROCESS THAT DELETES STORED OUTLINES!

Eventually, stored outlines will likely fall into disuse, but in the meantime, there are some important traps to avoid. In particular, exercise caution if you import stored outlines that have been customized to add sql hints.

The hints for outlines are referenced in two different tables, OL$ and OL$HINTS. One of the tables has the actual hints, and the other table has the *count* of the number of hints.

Here's where the trouble is: When you customize a stored outline by adding hints, the count will likely not match anymore. Upon import, the database will check the outlines imported, and compare the actual number of hints, to what the count is. If they don't match, out goes the outline!

Here's a simple script to check the hintcount, and build a script that you can use to correct the hintcount:

```
with pre as (
SELECT OL_NAME, COUNT(*) HINTCOUNT_SHOULD_BE
FROM OUTLN.OL$HINTS B  WHERE OL_NAME LIKE
'SQL%FIX'
GROUP BY OL_NAME
minus
SELECT OL_NAME, HINTCOUNT
FROM OUTLN.OL$
where ol_name like 'SQL%FIX'
)
select 'UPDATE OUTLN.OL$ SET HINTCOUNT =
'||HINTCOUNT_SHOULD_BE ||
' WHERE OL_NAME = '''||OL_NAME ||''';'
FROM PRE
/
```

EXEC #6 EASY WAY TO CREATE A SQL PROFILE

Sql profiles use an interesting method to improve performance. Sql profiles work because they have the luxury of expending enormous amounts of CPU time investigating different plan options, and gleaning better statistics. They use the same optimizer that presumably produced the poor execution plan in the first place—but they spend a lot more time to glean more information in order to optimizer the execution path.

There is a subtle difference between stored outlines and sql profiles. A stored outline uses a set of sql hints that tend to preserve certain steps in an execution plan (e.g., sql hints such as "full" or "index.") A sql profile, on the other hand uses hints that give the optimizer *extra information that it normally would not have.*

Let's see how it works.

Step 1: Create the Tuning Task
```
Declare
  L_Sql_Tune_Task_Id  Varchar2(100);
Begin
  L_Sql_Tune_Task_Id :=
Dbms_Sqltune.Create_Tuning_Task (
  Sql_Id      => '5k2b3qsy3b30r',
  Scope       =>
Dbms_Sqltune.Scope_Comprehensive,
  Time_Limit  => 60,
  Task_Name   => 'chris1',
  Description => 'chris1 ');
  Dbms_Output.Put_Line('L_Sql_Tune_Task_Id: ' ||
L_Sql_Tune_Task_Id);
End;
/
```

Step 2: Run The Tuning Task
```
Begin
  Dbms_Sqltune.Execute_Tuning_Task( Task_Name =>
'chris1' );
End;
/
```

Step 3: Get Recommendations

Let's see what Oracle has found:

```
Set Long 9999
Set Longchunksize 1000
Set Linesize 100
Select Dbms_Sqltune.Report_Tuning_Task(
'chris1')
  From Dual;
```

This could be a long report—it will show the sql, and include a summary of recommendations.

Step 4: Apply The Profile

Okay, let's activate the profile:

```
execute
dbms_sqltune.accept_sql_profile(task_name =>
'chris1', replace => TRUE);
```

EXEC #7 SETUP SQL PROFILES TO HANDLE LITERALS

One interesting facet of sql profiles, in contrast to stored outlines, is that a profile can work even if different literals are used. Of course, this is where a stored outline falls down.

The argument, *Force_Match* should be used to enable this feature, as shown here:

```
execute dbms_sqltune.accept_sql_profile(task_name =>
'chris1', -
replace => TRUE, force_match => TRUE);
```

EXEC #8 COPY SQL PROFILE TO ANOTHER DATABASE

Sql Profiles are really easy to use. Sometimes, we need to transfer a bunch of profiles to another database. This will work fine, as long as the other database is running the identical sql. Here's how to do it.

Create the special staging table

```
BEGIN
DBMS_SQLTUNE.CREATE_STGTAB_SQLPROF
(table_name => 'PROFILES', schema_name=>'CHRIS');
     END;
/
```

Copy desired profile to the Staging table

```
BEGIN
DBMS_SQLTUNE.PACK_STGTAB_SQLPROF
(profile_name           => 'SYS_SQLPROF_0659e1f0f6d80000',
staging_table_name => 'PROFILES',
staging_schema_owner=>'CHRIS');
END;
/
```

Make sure profile is there

```
select distinct obj_name from CHRIS.PROFILES;
```

Export special staging table

```
expdp cxly dumpfile=profiles.dmp TABLES=CHRIS.PROFILES
-- Dump file in
/u01/app/oracle/product/12.1.0/db_1/rdbms/log/profiles.d
mp
```

In Target Database Create Staging Table

```
BEGIN
DBMS_SQLTUNE.CREATE_STGTAB_SQLPROF
(table_name => 'PROFILES', schema_name=>'CHRIS');
     END;
/
```

Now import the profile

```
impdp cxly dumpfile=profiles.dmp TABLES=CHRIS.PROFILES
TABLE_EXISTS_ACTION=REPLACE
```

Transfer SQL profiles from Staging Table to Final place

```
BEGIN
DBMS_SQLTUNE.UNPACK_STGTAB_SQLPROF`
(staging_table_name => 'PROFILES',
staging_schema_owner=>'CHRIS', replace=>FALSE);
END;
/
```

Check to make sure new profile is there

```
COL NAME FORMAT A33
WAY select name, created from dba_sql_profiles order by
created;
```

EXEC #9 CREATE SQL PROFILE BASED ON HISTORICAL EXECUTION PLAN

Performance tuning specialists have many tools at their disposal. For example, I have used stored outlines and sql profiles many times. Each has some advantages. I normally use stored outlines to change an execution plan without any need to actually re-code anything.
Stored Outlines have one specific disadvantage, however, which I suspect is not widely known.

When you invoke an outline, the optimizer will *strip off any parallel hints* in the sql. Thus, if you need parallelism, an outline will not be a good choice.

Sql profiles, on the other hand do not remove parallelism. I have used profiles many times as well, but I have found the Sql Tuning Advisor, on which they are based, to be "hit or miss." In my experience, it is very common for a Sql Tuning Set to offer no good suggestions, or even fail to complete any useful analysis.

There is an overlooked tool, developed by Carlos Sierra, formerly of Oracle's *Center of Excellence*, that offers some special benefits. With this tricky, but simple to use script, you can create a sql profile, built on *any historical plan that is available*.

The script looks in dba_hist_sql_plan to grab the plan that you are want to use. Before you run this script, decide which Plan Hash Value you want for your Sql_id. You can check the performance of the various plans by querying *Dba_Hist_SqlStat*.

```
Select Snap_Id, Instance_Number,
Plan_Hash_Value, Px_Servers_Execs_Delta ,
Executions_Delta, Rows_Processed_Delta,
Round(Elapsed_Time_Delta/1000/(Executions_Delta+.01
),1) Timepermsec,
Round(Disk_Reads_Delta) Disk
From Dba_Hist_Sqlstat S
Where Sql_Id = [TBD]    Order By 1;
```

Once you have the PHV ready, you are ready to go! When you execute the script, it will prompt for a Sql_id. Then, it will display the various Plan Hash Values that are available in the historical plan tables. You select one of these plans; then, the script automatically figures out the hints that are needed, and creates a custom sql profile that uses those hints.

I recently had a performance tuning issue where the sql at one time had run well, but not anymore. The sql invoked parallelism, so that nixed the idea of a stored outline. Running the usual Sql Tuning set brought up no practical suggestions.

At this point, I remembered this script and gave it a try. I used this script and it worked perfectly. In about 1 minute, I had a correct, active sql profile that worked perfectly! Amazingly simple.

You run the script like this (you can optionally provide the sql_id and PHV) to avoid being prompted for these values:

`@coe_xfr_sql_profile.sql`

In just a few seconds, the hints will be ready. Then, you run a script of this form:

`@coe_xfr_sql_profile_[sqlid]_[phv].sql`

Although the script is packaged with SQLT, you can run the script as a standalone. Here is the actual script. I was delighted to find that it runs fine on my client; I did not need to transfer it to the server.

Even though the script mentions running as Sysdba, I found that running this script with my usual DBA account worked fine. Carlos reminds the user that you need to have the proper license to use Oracle's Tuning Pack.

So all in all, I think this script does a great job of solving some tough performance issues. Hats off to Carlos for doing the hard work to develop this tool.

EXEC #10 EASY WAYS TO INFLUENCE JOINS

It is sometimes necessary to prompt the optimizer to use a different join order. This is accomplished through *SQL hints*. These hints are actually embedded in a comment clause at the beginning of the SQL statement.

For tuning joins, here are several of the most commonly used SQL hints. Each of the following hints prompts the optimizer to use the specified join method:

```
Use_Nl
Use_Hash
```

The syntax for each hint is very simple (and similar). To suggest that the optimizer use a certain join method, the appropriate clause is inserted into a SQL comment, with the table names listed afterwards. For a nested loop, the following syntax would be used.

```
Select /*+USE_NL (TABLE_NAME1 TABLE_NAME2
TABLE_NAME3 . . . ) */
```

Similarly, the syntax for the other join is:

```
Select /*+USE_HASH (TABLE_NAME1 TABLE_NAME2
TABLE_NAME3 . . . ) */
```

If more than one table is included in the hint, simply list the table names or aliases one after the other, with no intervening punctuation. In the following SQL, we desired to use the sort merge join method on the *Customer* and *Overdue* tables; note that the table alias is used in the hint—not the actual table name:

```
SELECT /*+Use_Hash (C O) */
Cust_Name, Phone, DVD_Name,
From Customer C, Overdue O
WHERE C.Cust_Id = O.Cust_Id
AND Due_Date = '05-Jan-2002';
```

Another very useful hint is the *ORDERED* hint. It is often used in conjunction with another hint that suggests a join method. The syntax for this hint is very simple; no table names or other argument are specified at all:

```
Select /*+ORDERED */
```

The ordered hint simply requests that the optimizer join the tables in the specific order listed in the *from* clause. (Note that this is the opposite of the convention used in the old Rule Based Optimizer approach, in which the tables tended to join in the opposite order listed.)

When typing hints, note that the case for the hints may be either upper or lower case; the optimizer doesn't care.

Hints Pitfalls

Be sure to specify the alias name in the hint if the table listed in the SQL *from* clause makes use of an alias. Observe the hint syntax for the following SQL:

```
SELECT /*+Use_NL (C D) */
Cust_Name
From Customer C, Department D
WHERE C.Cust_Id = D.Cust_Id
AND Dept_Name = 'Engineering';
```

The SQL above correctly uses the two table aliases—C and D.

Be aware that using incorrect syntax in a hint will not always be easy to discover. Many analysts and DBAs have spent hours wondering why the optimizer is not "obeying" the hint, only to discover some typo in the hint syntax. In case of wrong syntax or "typos," the optimizer will simply ignore the hint--but you will not know!

EXEC #11 SIMPLE WAY TO CHANGE JOIN ORDER

There are several equally good ways to switch join order using sql hints.

Firstly, you can use the *Leading* sql hint to specify the leading table. In the following sql, we want *Table1* to start the join:

```
Select /*+Leading(T1) */
* from Table1 T1, Table2 T2
where T1.Emp_Id = T2.Emp_Id
and T1.Name like '%Smith%'
and T2.Dept like '%Engineering%';
```

Alternatively, you can use the *Ordered* hint, which, together with the order of tables in the *from* clause, specifies the join order for all the tables. In the following sql, we want Table2 to start the join, so we put it first after the keyword *from*.

```
Select /*+Ordered*/
* from Table2 T2, Table1 T1
where T1.Emp_Id = T2.Emp_Id
and T1.Name like '%Smith%'
and T2.Dept like '%Engineering%';
```

When using sql hints, always be sure to use the *alias*, if one is specified. If you don't use the alias, your hint will be ignored.

TIPS ON RAC, CLUSTERS, REPLICATION

In this section I provide some tips on dealing with RAC, as well as replication.

CLUSTER #1 HOW TO CHECK GOLDENGATE LAG TIME

In all types of replication, a common question is, "How far are we behind?" In GoldenGate, there are several simple ways to check lag. Both give the same information--just in different formats. In each case, first start the GoldenGate utility, ***ggsci***.

Method 1: *Lag* Command

Using this method requires that you first log into the database.

```
> lag *

Sending GETLAG request to EXTRACT EXT1TEST ...
Last record lag 4 seconds.
Sending GETLAG request to REPLICAT REP1TESTP ...
Last record lag 245 seconds.
Sending GETLAG request to REPLICAT REP2TESTP ...
Last record lag 1,720 seconds.
Sending GETLAG request to REPLICAT REP3TESTP ...
Last record lag 1,303 seconds.
Sending GETLAG request to REPLICAT REP4TESTP ...
Last record lag 785 seconds.
```

Method 2: *Info* Command

With this command, you don't actually need to be connected to the database.

```
> info all
```

Program	Status	Group	Lag at Chkpt	Time Since Chkpt
MANAGER	RUNNING			
JAGENT	STOPPED			
EXTRACT	RUNNING	EXT1TEST	00:00:05	00:00:04
REPLICAT	RUNNING	REP2TESTP	00:56:41	00:00:00
REPLICAT	RUNNING	REP3TESTP	00:43:24	00:00:00
REPLICAT	RUNNING	REP4TESTP	00:25:33	00:00:00

In both methods, you are given the lag time for each replicat. In the case shown here, we have 4 replicats. You can see that replicat REP2TESTP and REP3TESTP are each lagging nearly an hour.

CLUSTER #2 MEASURE RAC CACHE INTERNODE TIME

The Overhead of Running RAC

Each RAC cluster relies on a fast private interconnect amongst the nodes in the cluster. Blocks needed by one node can quickly be sent from a node already having that block cached. This is called "Cache Fusion."

There IS a cost to sending these blocks around the nodes; the transmission is not instantaneous, and in some cases can actually become a bottleneck.

Of course, the modern Cache Fusion is FAR faster than the old days of OPS, where a block had to be written to disk by one node, then read by another node. That "ping" could easily cause a 10 ms delay just for one block. Well, we are much better now!

If you check the AWR report for a node on your cluster, you can see the sql that are slowed by cluster time. On the large systems I have analyzed, some sql are slowed by 10% or more due to these delays.

It is not unusual to blame "the network" for RAC performance issues. The only problem with that idea is that it's often tough to prove. So, how does one figure out how fast your Cache Fusion really is?

An Easy Way to Measure Cache Fusion

Here is an easy way to check the RAC internode time. One of the quickest events that Oracle uses to communicate is called the "2-way gc grant." It's normally very fast (typically 1 ms or less.) This is similar to a fast network "ping."

Here's the key point: Just think of what would happen if the time to send a block in the cluster took much longer than 1 ms. We can get an historical chart, sorted by snapshot, of this fast "grant" event.

```
WITH BASE AS (SELECT instance_number, SNAP_ID,
TOTAL_WAITS, time_waited_micro/1000 timemsec,
 LAG(time_waited_micro/1000, 1) OVER (ORDER BY snap_id)
```

```
AS PREV_TIME_MSEC,
 LAG(total_waits, 1) OVER (ORDER BY snap_id) AS
PREV_waits
FROM dba_hist_system_event
WHERE event_name ='gc cr grant 2-way'
and instance_number = 1
and snap_id between tbd and tbd
)
SELECT b.SNAP_ID, b.instance_number NODE,
to_char(begin_interval_time, 'dd-mon-yy-hh24:mi') BEG,
 (TOTAL_WAITS-PREV_WAITS) "#WAITS",
ROUND((TIMEMSEC-PREV_TIME_MSEC)/(.001+TOTAL_WAITS-
PREV_WAITS), 1) "RATE" FROM BASE b,
dba_hist_snapshot S
where b.instance_number = s.instance_number
andb.snap_id = s.snap_id
and (total_waits-prev_waits) > 99900
ORDER BY 1;
```

In the above script, I use an analytical function, "Lag" to find the difference shown in 2 rows of the table.

Expected Output

On most systems I analyze, the internode time is 1 ms or less. In the output below, you can see that the internode time is rock-steady at just .3 ms. In my experience, that is about the best possible.

SNAP_ID	NODE	BEG	#WAITS	RATE
17236	7	13-apr-09-05:00	1942375	.3
17237	7	13-apr-09-06:00	1913682	.3
17238	7	13-apr-09-07:00	3763238	.3
17239	7	13-apr-09-08:00	2360403	.4
17240	7	13-apr-09-09:00	1694804	.3
17241	7	13-apr-09-10:00	1564779	.3
17242	7	13-apr-09-11:00	551387	.3

On a well-designed system, the interconnect rate doesn't change much. I typically see a few spikes to about 1.5 ms, but that's about it.

In the script above, be sure to put in your own snapshot_id's. Also, you may want to check the internode performance among all the nodes--not just node 1, as shown in the script above.

CLUSTER #3 OVERHEAD FOR RAC IS SMALL (BUT NOT ZERO)

Occasionally, marketing folks, in their zeal, suggest that RAC will actually make things go *faster*. Of course, that's really not true. Using RAC doesn't somehow make things work faster. What the marketers really mean is that the overall throughout of your application will be larger if your application is strictly CPU-limited, and simply needs more processing power. Thus, RAC provides the opportunity to increase the number of threads run concurrently.

We must always remember, however, there are numerous other bottlenecks that must be considered as well. For example, you might actually be experiencing waits due to available log buffers. In this scenario, adding more CPUs would be counterproductive.

RAC cannot make an application scale, if it otherwise would not. As Oracle's Admin Guide states, "If an application does not scale on an SMP system, then moving the application to an Oracle RAC database cannot improve performance."

Let's take a look at the overhead due to cache fusion. These statistics come from a very large database, on an 8-node cluster. In particular, let's look at one very busy node, which handles OLTP queries. For a recent 24-hour period, let's see what the top wait events were. We'll use the familiar AWR report to glean this information:

```
Top-5 wait events for a 24-hour period:

db file sequential read     277k secs
CPU time                    140k secs
gc current block 3-way       24k secs
gc cr grant 2-way            16k secs
log file sync                 8k secs
```

The above chart confirms that RAC-specific events, while certainly noticeable, aren't anywhere close to being the top-wait events. Roughly speaking, they amount to about 15% of the total wait time.

So, it's worth remembering that performance issues on a single-node systems won't magically go away once RAC is installed. If anything, performance issues are intensified unless you actually resolve the underlying issues.

Does RAC really cause degradation of 15%?

I don't think so—here's why: The above RAC wait events—while indeed true delays—are occurring so that *even greater delays will be avoided*. The inter-node block transfers are occurring in order to avoid disk reads.

With RAC, we have a multi-node, monstrous-sized cache, and another node has the desired block cached. So, we do a little work (block transfer) to *avoid* bigger work (disk reads).

In practice, on very large RAC systems, I have found that Oracle spends roughly 1 ms getting a block in order to avoid spending 5 ms for a single block read (sequential read.) On the complex RAC systems I have used, there have been very few cases where being on RAC has been the actual root cause of a performance problem.

CLUSTER #4 FIND SESSIONS ON ALL RAC NODES

If you work on RAC clusters, you will find this script useful. It gives you a tidy summary of all active sessions, across all nodes.

Live many RAC scripts, it starts with switching the view name to the "GV" type of view.

```
Select Inst_Id Inst, Sid, Module,
Event,(Sysdate-Sql_Exec_Start)*24*60*60 Secs,
Logon_Time,Sql_Id
From GV$Session
where type != 'BACKGROUND'
and event not like 'SQL*Net%' and
       event not like 'Streams AQ: waiting%'
and event not like 'PL/SQL lock timer%'
and event not like 'PX Deq%'
and event not like 'jobq%'
and module not like 'Gol%';
```

In the above script, I don't want to see any background processes, or the parallel slaves ("PX...")

Similarly, I don't' want to see any Sql*Net idle processes.

CLUSTER #5 FIND LONG-RUNNING SESSIONS ON ANY NODE

Naturally, a DBA wants to spot a long-running sessions. But what if you're on RAC—how do you do that?

Here's an one way to home-in on the problem session. The script below identifies user sessions, across all nodes, that have been connected for at least 8 hours.

Keep in mind, however, that a long-connected session is not necessarily a problem, especially if a connection pool is being used:

```
Col Sid Format 99999
Col Serial# Format 999999
Col Machine Format A15 Truncate
Col Event Format A30 Truncate
Col Inst Format 9999

Select Inst_Id Inst, Sid, Serial#,Username,
Machine,Event,
Logon_Time,Sql_Id,Prev_Sql_Id
From Gv$Session
where type != 'BACKGROUND'  and event not like
'SQL*Net%'
   and event not like 'Streams AQ: waiting%'
   And Nvl(24 * (Sysdate - Logon_Time),0) > 8
Order By Username;
```

WILD & WISE TACTICS

In this section, I detail some "different" ideas. Some are pretty mild, but others are really zany ideas. These are not just theoretical suggestions—these are tactics I have personally used, and they *work*. Nevertheless, they are not the first thing you should try.

Tried to Change an "init.ora" parameter.

WILD #1 WHEN ALL ELSE FAILS: MAGIC PERFORMANCE BOOST

A major retailer had a problem with a long-running batch job. We were able to identify several bottlenecks; unfortunately, the fix required a program redesign; however, this was not acceptable. Along with QA testing and all the paperwork, the ensuing delay would be at least several weeks, if not a month or more.

I considered all kinds of crazy ideas—server changes, init.ora changes, disk changes, etc. Finally, I thought of one very simple, but admittedly *weaselly* idea. Since the bottleneck was mostly due to disk I/o, any improvement in disk access would directly affect the problem job. Since we knew the exact Sql, we could pre-run Sql that duplicated the "real" Sql that would shortly follow. That is, we would *pre-cache* many of the blocks that would shortly be needed.

Caching would take place within the SAN unit, as well as at the Oracle database cache. The entire performance improvement would take place with absolutely no change to the batch program!

Here's an important key: To speed-up the pre-caching program, we used multi-threading to run about 20 simultaneous database sessions (we had the spare CPU capacity).

We successfully ran the "Boost" program just prior to the problem batch job, reducing the runtime by several hours. This satisfied the short-term needs of the client. (Incidentally, I have used this "boost" idea several other times, where an urgent, short-term fix was required.)

WILD #2 FIND SQL THAT ARE "INVISIBLE"

It's usually easy to find long-running sql. For one thing, they show up in the first section of a typical AWR report. The cumulative runtime for all executions of problem sql are clearly shown in the "Elapsed Time" section. They will often show up in other sections as well, such as the Disk I/O or Buffer Gets sections. So normally, this is a trivial step.

But what if the application doesn't use bind variables? In that case, there isn't any "cumulative runtime," since each sql has a different sql_id. In these cases, the sql *will not show up anywhere* in the AWR report. How can you spot these?

How to Spot Invisible Sql

It turns out that these evasive sql are easy to find. Here's the key: The sql statement uses the same amount of memory, even though the literal values change. Knowing this, you can do a simple query that identifies statements that have the same *form*. Here's how I do it:

```
Select Persistent_Mem, Count(*) From V$Sql
Group By Persistent_Mem Having Count(*) > 1000
Order by 2;
```

PERSISTENT_MEM	COUNT(*)
8728	1251
1712	1621
7176	81406

Notice that in the above example, there is one form (Persistent_Mem = 7176) that is apparently run a huge amount of times. Now, run another query to identify the culprit (and cut-off at just a first few rows):

```
Select Sql_Text From V$Sql
Where Persistent_mem = 7176 and RowNum < 5;
```

Once you have identified the culprit(s), you can easily "roll-up" the statistics for all sql having that Persistent_Mem. You will never be fooled again!

WILD #3 USE PARALLELISM "BACKWARDS"

There's another option that seems bizarre at first, but works incredibly well. It requires using Oracle parallelism in a strange way. With this scheme, we can avoid the full scan used by the hash join, while bypassing the inefficiencies intrinsic with the nested-loop method.

Assume we have a need to extract details for all sales for all products starting with the name "BEARING". To accomplish this, we query two tables: PRODUCTS and SALES. Table SALES (1 billion rows) stores all transactions for the last 3 years. Table PRODUCTS (10,000 rows) is the list of all sellable products.

Here's our query:

```
Select S.Sale_Amt,
S.Discount, S.Emp_Discount, S.Clerk, S.Tax,
S.Register, S.Timestamp, S.Store
From PRODUCTS P, SALES S
Where P.part_no = S.Part_No
And P.Part_ Name like 'BEARING%'
```

We estimate that the above query will return roughly 1 million rows (100 products x 10,000 sales.) Note that this result set is only about 0.1% of the SALES table. We can assume that the table SALES has an index that matches the join condition (Part_No).

Let's review the nested-loop method. The reason it performs so poorly is that it is *single threaded*. In a nested loop, one session works on a single row at a time. But what if we could expand the nested loop method so that it did lots of nested loop joins all at the same time? One way to invoke this "multithreading" would be to somehow divide the table by key values, then manually start a bunch of Sql*Plus sessions to share the work. Then, we would combine the result sets.

It turns out that there's a simpler way to initiate multithreading--using Oracle parallelism. In this approach, Oracle automatically starts up separate sessions, just like with the hash join. But now, the sessions are all doing nested loop joins.

Here's the SQL hint to use Oracle parallelism to start multi-threading:

```
Select /*+parallel (P 30) Use_Nl (P S) */
```

The key of this technique is that we specify the parallelism on the *Product* table--that is the *small* table! That's because we want all the processes to begin on that table, as we did for our regular nested-loop join. Note that this is the *opposite* of what we normally do with Oracle Parallelism, where the parallel hint goes on the huge table.

We have another change as well: We specify the *Use_Nl* hint. This ensures that Oracle doesn't perform a hash join. With multithreading, we want the nested-loop method.

Surprisingly, tests show that we can successfully launch a huge number of threads without contention. The optimum number is far more than the parallelism degree we normally specify. Also, whereas regular parallelism normally launches processes equal to twice the degree specified (one set for reading; one set for processing results), this new method launches fewer processes-- just 1x the degree.

Sample tests confirm that using 30 threads (or more) on a server with 8 CPUs works nicely. We don't quite get 30x improvement, but close. The actual measured gain is about 25x. For our sample case here, that means a runtime of 10 minutes

WILD #4 PRETEND PERFORMANCE IS *A MATTER OF LIFE OR DEATH*

I bet this is the craziest tip you have ever seen. Performance tuning requires creativity and innovation. It's not at all just a routine, drab job—it requires versatility and stepping into different roles. That's why I like it so much.

Those not truly experienced in tuning tend to trivialize the process, frequently using trite phrases such as "add missing indexes" or "increase buffer cache." This misunderstanding helps explain why relatively few DBAs become really good at performance tuning—their view of the task is simply too short-sighted. If your solution set comprises only trivial solutions like new indexes, you're likely not going to excel in this field.

Here's a tactic I use when I'm faced with an apparently unsolvable performance problem. I imagine that the problem is so critical that people will actually *die* if I don't resolve the difficulty. I imagine that the lives of people are actually in my hands.

Yes, I admit this is a bizarre idea, but it actually works. If you can temporarily pretend that there are no limits, you'll be amazed at the variety of solutions you can invent.

WILD #5 BUILD A NETWORK OF ORACLE PROFESSIONALS

This tip is not really a technical tip, but it's one of the most valuable suggestions I can offer. On more than one occasion, I have mentioned a (supposedly) difficult problem to a colleague, only to hear the problem solved instantly. Instead of hearing sympathy about how difficult my problem is, I get a *solution*! The point is, what oftentimes looks terribly difficult to one person appears *trivial* to another.

No One Person Knows it All

Given the huge variety of database issues, it is not reasonable to hope that any one DBA can possibly "know it all." Each Oracle analyst possesses a special set of expertise, along with a background different than anyone else.

This wide variety of experience means that a skillful analyst, by nurturing a growing list of contacts, can theoretically "consult" with many experts on almost any conceivable database issue. It really doesn't make any difference who "really" knows the answer, or who gets "credit" for it; the important thing is to efficiently locate the information needed to solve your customer's performance problem.

Besides your immediate place of business, these contacts can be made through the local Oracle user groups. These groups frequently feature speakers of national reputation and expertise.

Another possibility for Oracle networking is the various Internet forums, such as national Oracle groups, as well as "Open World." Other discussion forums can be found at the web sites of the larger software and hardware vendors. These web sites often include white papers, "lessons learned," and other research articles of interest.

By cultivating a list of contacts, you will soon find that you have a generated a mini network of valuable consultants with whom you can share information. This sort of networking arrangement is just a smart career move, and could easily lead to your next challenging assignment. Also, don't be surprised if one of your network "consultants" has an immediate solution to your next "really tough problem."

WILD #6 WATCH OUT! AWR REPORTS REMOVE EXTRA WHITESPACE

I got burned on this one at least once. Sometimes, you need to have the exact sql—for example, if you are creating a stored outline. Most of the time, "whitespace" between clauses or keywords is not relevant. But sometimes it is critical.

What if the extra blanks occur as part of the *functionality* of the sql? That is, it's not just "whitespace," but something pertinent to the actual functionality of the code.

My code had a clause like this:

```
Where col1 like '%      abc      %'
```

In the AWR/Sql report, it was altered to look like this:

```
Where col1 like '%abc%'
```

I tried to create a stored outline on the sql, but it wouldn't work, no matter how often I dropped/recreated. The problem of course, was the missing blanks. Once I saw what had happened, I simply altered the outline script to add back extra blanks

WILD #7 USE QUERY SUBFACTORING INSTEAD OF INLINE VIEWS

This is sometimes called the "With" syntax, because that's exactly how the Sql begins. Query subfactoring is very similar to using an inline view, except that the subfactor is put at the very front of the query. Then, the main body of your sql can read from it, just like a view.

This syntax is often used to make a complicated query more readable. In many cases, you could use inline views instead, but that would likely be more cumbersome for others to review.

Here's an example of query subfactoring:

```
With Part1 as
(Select * from Emp
Where Emp_Name like '%SMITH%')
(Select Count(*)
from Part1);
```

In this simple example, *Part1* is the subfactor. Although this example only has a single subfactor (*Part1*), you can include many subfactors up front (but you don't repeat the *With* keyword)

When you use query subfactoring, Oracle may either temporarily store the subfactor data in a global temporary table, or it may re-retrieve the data each time it is needed. This can have a big performance impact, especially on a very busy OLTP system, so you may need to carefully test each method. (You can see when Oracle builds a global temp table in the trace file.)

You can control how the optimizer handles the subfactor with these sql hints:

WILD #8 FOR HUGE SETS, CHANGE NUMBER OF ROWS SENT PER TRIP

In sql*plus parameter is called *arraysize*. It specifies how many rows to return to the client each time. This greatly impacts how many network roundtrips will be required when retrieving data. By reducing the number of network trips, overall runtime can be substantially reduced.

When transferring large amounts of data, the default setting (15) is likely not optimum. You can experiment with larger values (up to 5000) and watch the sql*net roundtrips decline. Using sql*plus *autotrace* is an easy way to do this.

Keep in mind that performance improvement will fall off drastically once the arraysize has been increased. Again, trial and error with your particular data set is a good idea.

Here's how you change the setting:

```
SQL> arraysize 1000
```

Here is how you check the current setting:

```
SQL> show arraysize
arraysize 15
```

For applications other than Sql*Plus, they are sometimes able to make a similar change. I've found that if you explain what you are trying to do, the application expert can often accommodate you.

WILD #9 STRANGE DELAYS IN FLASHBACK QUERY

Despite the appealing name, "flashback," a flashback query can run very slowly. On a large production system, a flashback query going back a few hours can easily take 10 hours. What--how can that be?

This happens because Oracle must reconstruct an object as it existed at a certain time. This is the same idea of read-consistency. This reconstruction happens one block at a time, going backwards in time, undoing each transaction.

Starting the Undo

There are other issues with a flashback query that make the process run even slower. Of course, Oracle does indeed save the undo information-- we can certainly find it, and a flashback query really does work. Here's the problem: The structure of undo segments is heavily biased towards quickly *saving* transaction information--not quickly *reversing* transactions.

Before Oracle can reconstruct an object, it has to *identify* what needs to be undone. One would think this is a trivial step, but not so. This can be very time-consuming--especially when the database has undergone lots of recent transactions.

Transaction Table

In each undo segment header there lies a critical structure known as the *transaction table*. It's not a "table" as we normally think of it. Maybe a "list" would have been a better name. The transaction table identifies the undo information held in that undo segment. For example, any given entry points to where to find the actual undo block.

That sounds excellent, but the entire transaction table only has information for 34 transactions. (Yes, that sounds small to me, too.) Each entry is called a transaction *slot*. As more transactions are housed in a given undo segment, transaction slots, being so few, are very often *overwritten*. The information is not lost, of course, but to find it, several extra steps will be required. On a very busy system, it could take thousands of extra reads just to find where to start. (That's why I

---

observed that Oracle seems very biased towards going forward with the undo, not actually applying it.)

Remember--all this effort is before Oracle even starts the "real work" of rebuilding the object of interest to the time desired. Of course, that final step will add even more time. The point is, the delay of determining where to start can be vastly more than the work required to actually *do* the reconstructing of the object.

Troubleshooting

Troubleshooting a flashback query delay is not so easy. On a busy system, I have seen flashback queries require *millions* of extra reads to flashback a small table with only 20,000 transactions that needed to be undone. If you query the active session history for the session of interest, it will show that it is performing sequential reads from an undo tablespace. One could easily be fooled into thinking (as I did) that there must have been a huge number of transactions on the table of interest. We know better now--the reads were actually Oracle synthesizing the undo information in the transaction table, not actually applying it to the object of interest.

When a transaction table slot is reused, what happens to the valuable information that used to be kept in that slot? Well, there's one logical place for it to go--somewhere in undo-land. In fact, Oracle stores the old slot information right at the beginning of the new undo block that used that slot. In this way, the information is linked together. Therefore, when we perform a flashback query, we can discover what the transaction table looked like at some prior state.

Undoing the Undo?

Hey, what a minute--all this almost sounds like "undoing the undo!" You're right, and Oracle calls it, "Transaction Table Rollback." You can also get a summary in the AWR report, in the *Instance Activity* section.

You can also quantify this event in real time, to get a feel for how often this is happening. On a busy system, it is likely happening all the time. Let's see how we do this on a busy RAC system. Here is one way to see this occurring in the current connected sessions. This would be helpful to know if someone is doing a flashback query that seems to be running far longer than expected.

In this script, I look for large values of transaction table undo, and list the sessions. I also ignore the background processes (that's why I exclude programs like 'oracle'):

```
Col Module Format A22
Col Sid Format 99999
Col Program Format A20
Col Inst Format 9999
Col Trundo Format 9999999

Select One.Inst_Id INST, One.Sid, Substr(Program,1,20)
PROG,
Substr(Module,1,20) Mod, Value TRUNDO
From Gv$Sesstat One, V$Statname Two, Gv$Session Three
Where One.Statistic# = Two.Statistic#
And One.Inst_Id = Three.Inst_Id
And One.Sid = Three.Sid
And Name =
'transaction tables consistent reads - undo records
applied'
And Program Not Like 'Oracle@%'
And Value > 90000
Order By Value;
```

What can I do?

The essence of the problem is having to repeatedly reconstruct the contents of the "slots" in the transaction table. If there were fewer re-uses of the slots, then there would be less work required. Oracle support has suggested keeping more undo segments online--and therefore more slots available.

This is accomplished by setting the underscore parameter, *_rollback_segment_count*. The idea is, to override the automatic undo process, and force more undo segments to stay online. It seems like the number of reused "slots" should go down commensurate with the extra undo segments that are kept online. So, if we keep 4x as many undo segments online, I would expect to see approximately a 4x reduction in transaction table rollbacks. That's the theory, anyway, but I haven't confirmed that yet.

WILD #10 DIFFERENT EXECUTION PLAN CAN HAVE *SAME* PHV

This one really surprised me, and upset some assumptions I had made. See if you are as surprised as I was. Here's a simple sql I was working on:

```
Select 'X' From Tab1 T1 Where Code = 'xyz'
--
And Exists (Select 'X' From Tab2 T2 --CLAUSE 1
Where T2.Op_Id = T1.Op_Id And T2.Flg= 'a'
--
And Exists (Select 'X' From Tab2 T2 --CLAUSE 2
Where T2.Op_Id = T1.Op_Id And T2.Flg= 'b'
--
And Exists (Select 'X' From Tab2 T2 --CLAUSE 3
Where T2.Op_Id = T1.Op_Id And T2.Flg= 'b' ;
```

In the sql above, Oracle will first consider the main body, and then the three *Exists* clauses. Let's assume that the optimizer considers Clause 1, then Clause 2, then Clause 3. For the main body, the index used is *Tab1_Index*. For the subqueries, the index is called *Tab2_Index*.

The execution plan is simple—*Tab1* first, followed by the subqueries:

```
SELECT STATEMENT
NESTED LOOPS
NESTED LOOPS
NESTED LOOPS
NESTED LOOPS
TABLE ACCESS BY INDEX ROWID TAB1
INDEX RANGE SCAN TAB1_INDEX
TABLE ACCESS BY INDEX ROWID TAB2
INDEX RANGE SCAN TAB2_INDEX
TABLE ACCESS BY INDEX ROWID TAB2
INDEX RANGE SCAN TAB2_INDEX
TABLE ACCESS BY INDEX ROWID TAB2
INDEX RANGE SCAN TAB2_INDEX
```

Note that each *Exists* clause queries the same table—*Tab2*. In my actual case, It turns out that the order in which Oracle applies each Exists clause is critical to performance, because one of the clauses drastically reduces the result set. Yet you cannot tell by looking at the execution plan which clause is considered next. No matter which order Oracle applies the subqueries, *the plan will look exactly the same.*

In my particular case, it was critical for Clause 2 be considered before the other *Exists* clauses. That information cannot be gleaned from the execution plan.

Even Weirder

I thought at first that I was making some mistake, and that if I just looked at other columns in Plan_Table, I could detect a difference in the execution plans. Not so--the Plan Hash Value
(PHV) is identical in each execution plan, even though the optimizer is doing something different! I suppose this is consistent in a fashion, since the plan details displayed are indeed
identical in each case.

Admittedly, having the same PHV for different actions is a rarity. Other DBAs have done considerable research on the subject of plan hash values, and have uncovered many cases where different optimizer action yields the same PHV. Some examples: Sql using different degrees of parallelism, or different filtering criteria.

For busy OLTP systems, it's sometimes nice to quickly spot occasional queries that are running more than a few seconds. (For example, when a user omits search criteria.) Note that AWR reports may not be too useful in spotting the occasional OLTP outlier. These queries are typically not listed in AWR, as they consume such a small consumer of database resources. Thus, they often fly "under the radar."

WILD #11 WHEN INDEX ORDER DOESN'T MATTER

All DBAs are familiar with the guidelines regarding index usage. We all understand that we should build indexes on columns that are very discriminatory—that is, they help Oracle to isolate the result set as quickly as possible. In addition, we understand that the *leading columns* of an index should match the search criteria specified in your Sql.

Given the above guidelines, it only seems natural, then, to conclude that the most discriminating columns should be placed before the other columns in the index. It just seems obvious that starting with the most discriminating column must reduce the work, because Oracle can more efficiently discriminate if it begins with the "best" column first. This conclusion fits right in with our practice of "leading edge" columns in an index.

While it's true that the leading columns of the index must match the Sql criteria, once that condition is met, it doesn't make a difference which column comes first. Our intuition is flat-out wrong!

The essence of the issue is simply this: Once Oracle has qualified an index to be used, there is nothing magical about which column on the "left" side. Oracle's algorithm, when building (or traversing) a branch of a B*Tree, *combines* the relevant columns. It's the *composite* that is used to point to the next branch of the B*Tree, not just one column. So "left" or "right" has no particular benefit.

Consider the following indexes:

```
INDEX1: (ZIP_CODE, GENDER)
INDEX2: (GENDER, ZIP_CODE)
```

Assume we are looking for the combination of Zip_Code = 94568 and Gender = 'Male.' Before Oracle traverses the index, it combines the two conditions. The composite value, something like *94568_Male* has the same discriminatory value as *Male_94568*. That is, there is not magical about being on the left.

WILD #12 CREATE A LONG-TERM STATS REPOSITORY

This tip is one of the most powerful ideas I have ever used. Using the AWR repository is great if you only need to check back a month or two. But what if you want to see a long term trend over years? Suppose you want to see a sql has degraded over time?

Obviously, the AWR is not going to be very helpful; therefore, for some critical databases, we have created a repository that contains *years* of information. The beauty of this approach is, that you only need a small set of tables, which don't require a lot of disk space.

You don't really need the Active Session information—you just need the metrics for each sql. It is astonishing the information you can glean from just five tables. Here are our five custom tables:

```
DA_DBA_HIST_SERVICE_STAT
DA_DBA_HIST_SNAPSHOT
DA_DBA_HIST_SQLSTAT
DA_DBA_HIST_SYSSTAT
DA_DBA_HIST_SYSTEM_EVENT
```

A few times a day, we run a job that copies the new information from the original "Dba_Hist" tables into our repository. Then, to use these five tables, you simple query your repository tables instead, like this:

```
Select Snap_Id, Instance_Number,
Plan_Hash_Value,
Px_Servers_Execs_Delta ,
Executions_Delta, Rows_Processed_Delta,
Round(Disk_Reads_Delta) Disk
From Da.Da_Dba_Hist_Sqlstat S
Where Sql_Id = 'Tbd'
Order By 1;
```

WILD #13 RECOGNIZE QUERY BLOCK HINTS

A query block identifies a particular area of sql code, which can be distinguished from other parts—such as subqueries. This is useful to know for several reasons. Firstly, query blocks can be used in sql hints so that the hint just applies to certain parts of the sql (i.e., certain query blocks)

Secondly, query block syntax is used behind the scenes when Oracle builds stored outlines or sql profiles. When I first saw the code used in sql profiles, I was confused by the query block syntax. I didn't know what it was, but it's not that complicated. Once you understand the format of query blocks, the hints that you see in the stored outline or profile views will make sense.

Let's take a look at a simple sql statement to understand the concept. Consider the following query:

Select Ename From Scott.Emp Where Empno = 123;

There's really only one part to this query—so we would expect just one main query block. Let's do a simple *explain plan* query, but include this new field. The query block is available in the *Plan_Table*, column *Qblock_Name*.

```
Col Qblock_Name Format A15
Col Operation Format A20
Select Qblock_Name,      Id, Parent_Id,
Lpad (' ', Level - 1) || Operation || ' ' ||
            Options Operation, Object_Name
From        Plan_Table
Where       Statement_Id = '&Stmt_Id'
Start With Id = 0
And         Statement_Id = '&Stmt_Id'
Connect By Prior
            Id = Parent_Id
And         Statement_Id = '&Stmt_Id';


QBLOCK_NAME      ID PARENT OPERATION            OBJECT_NAME
--------------- ---- ------ -------------------- ----------------
                 0          SELECT STATEMENT
SEL$1            1      0   TABLE ACCESS BY IND  EMP
SEL$1            2      1     INDEX UNIQUE SCAN  PK_EMP
```

In the above results, note that a query block name, when automatically given by the optimizer, is of the form "SEL $n." So in our example, Oracle has called it, *SEL$1*. Note that the query block number assigned by Oracle will not always be so simple as 1,2,3, etc.

Query Blocks in Sql Profiles

Here's an example of how query blocks are used in sql profiles. The code below (actually a sql hint) is from a sql profile:

```
OPT_ESTIMATE(@"SEL$AF73C875", TABLE,
"S"@"SEL$4", SCALE_ROWS=3024)
```

We can now understand what this hint means. We see that the hint references two different query blocks— *SEL$AF73C875* and *SEL$4*. (The *Scale_Rows* parameter means to scale up (or down) the estimate of the rows to be returned.)

WILD #14 RECOGNIZE "EXTENDED" HINTS

Extended hints resemble normal sql hints—but they are more cryptic-looking. Here's are some examples of extended sql hints. These hints were used in some stored outlines I had created:

```
USE_NL(@"SEL$1"  "ABNQ"@"SEL$1")
LEADING(@"SEL$1"  "RQ4"@"SEL$1"  "ABO"@"SEL$1"
"V1D"@"SEL$1"  "XBL"@"SEL$1")
```

At first, the syntax looks bewildering, but based on what we learned about query blocks, we can get the gist of what the hints are doing, Most importantly, we know that the "@SEL$1" syntax is referring to a query block (explained in the prior section.) So most of the hints are being applied to query block *SEL$1*. So the optimizer is being instructed to join the tables (identified by their respective aliases) in the order shown.

If we look at the actual sql for the outline, we do indeed see those table aliases contained:

```
Select [List Of Fields]
From Vi_Data_Rgaf V1d,
Xvi_Md_Tbl Xbl,
Abo_Aoot_Obj Abo,
Vmti_Md_Cco_Tbl Rq4
Where  * * *
```

Clearly, the hint 's purpose is to ensure a certain join order. So, we can see that the extended hint makes sense.

Hints Similar, But a Little Different

In the prior tip, I illustrated some hints that were used in a sql profile:

```
OPT_ESTIMATE(@"SEL$AF73C875", TABLE,
"S"@"SEL$4", SCALE_ROWS=3024)
```

In this example, the optimizer is being instructed via the *Scale_Rows* keyword to change its cardinality estimate for a table by 3024. That is, the

Scale_Rows hint works similar to the *cardinality* hint—but uses a scaling factor instead.

Finding Extended Hints

Here's a way to see extended hints for particular sql of interest. In the *V$Sql* view, the field *Other_Xml* contains this hint information.

```
select extractvalue(value(d), '/hint')
as Ext_Hint
from xmltable('/*/outline_data/hint'
passing (
select xmltype(other_xml) as xmlval
from v$sql_plan
where sql_id='TBD'
and child_number = 0
and other_xml IS NOT NULL )) d
/

EXT_HINT
------------------------------------------
IGNORE_OPTIM_EMBEDDED_HINTS
OPTIMIZER_FEATURES_ENABLE('11.2.0.2')
DB_VERSION('11.2.0.2')
OPT_PARAM('optimizer_index_cost_adj' 1)
OPT_PARAM('optimizer_index_caching' 100)
```

WILD #15 "PUSH" SQL HINT EXPLAINED

The "Push" type of hints have always confused me, and I bet others have been confused as well. I hope this section clears things up.

I occasionally run into queries having multiple tables and clauses, in which I need the optimizer to evaluate certain clauses as early as possible—before joining to the other tables. Oracle provides a hint for doing this: *Push_Subq*. Naturally, there is also an inverse hint, *No_Push_Subq*. Accordingly to Oracle documentation, *No_Push_Subq* instructs the optimizer to evaluate the clause as late as feasible.

In Oracle hints, the term "push" is an awkward choice, and has always confused me. Here's the key: All it really means is, evaluate a section of code as *early as possible*. In other words, *push* it to the *front of the line*. Note that in Oracle versions prior to Oracle 10, the *Push_Subq* hint was applied to the entire sql statement. Beginning in Oracle 10, you can selectively decide which parts to push or not push.

Sample Query

Let's see how this works in practice I first create three simple tables. For purposes of our illustration, it is not important that they actually contain any data:

```
Create table parent  (id1 number, col2 number);
Create table child   (id1 number, col2 number);
Create table subtest (id1 number, col2 number, col3
number);
```

Now, let's create a query that has a main portion, and a subquery, that may be evaluated earlier, or later.

Select Par.Col2, Chi.Col2
From Parent Par, Child Chi
Where Par.Id1 Between 1001 And 2200
And Chi.Id1 = Par.Id1
And Exists (
Select /*+ No_Unnest Qb_Name(Subq1) */
'X' From Subtest Sub1
Where Sub1.Id1 = Par.Id1

And Sub1.Col2 = Par.Col2

And Sub1.Col3 >= '2')

In the query above, note that the optimizer has an option on when our subquery, *Subq1*, should be applied. It can join the parent and child tables, and then consider the clause afterwards; or it can evaluate the subquery earlier.

Also note that we included two hints, *No_Unnest*, and *Qb_Name*. The hint *No_Unnest* is used to prevent the optimizer from merging the subquery into the main body. This is a requirement for the *Push_Subq* hint to work.

Base Plan

In the base plan, without any "pushing" hints, the optimizer considers the subquery last.

QBLOCK_NAME	OPERATION	OBJECT_NAME
	SELECT STATEMENT	
SEL$1	**FILTER**	
	HASH JOIN	
SEL$1	TABLE ACCESS FULL	PARENT
SEL$1	TABLE ACCESS FULL	CHILD
SUBQ1	**TABLE ACCESS FULL**	**SUBTEST**

Notice that Oracle calls the subquery *SUBQ1*—exactly what we named it with our hint. There is one subtle, but very critical line in this plan--the *Filter* operation. This indicates that the subquery remains unnested—it hasn't been integrated into the main body of the sql. Again, that is mandatory for out pushing hint to be accepted by the optimizer.

Try Pushing

Now, let's assume we want the subquery to be evaluated soon. Let's apply the *Push_Subq* hint and see what happens.

```
Select /*+Push_Subq(@Subq1) */
    Par.Col2,Chi.Col2From Parent  Par, Child
Chi
Where Par.Id1 Between 1001 And 2200
And Chi.Id1 = Par.Id1
And Exists
```

```
   (Select /*+ No_Unnest Qb_Name(Subq1) */     '
   X' From     Subtest Sub1
   Where   Sub1.Id1 = Par.Id1
   And Sub1.Col2 = Par.Col2
   And Sub1.Col3 >= '2')
```

As expected, we see that the subquery has indeed moved up in the order.

```
QBLOCK_NAME     OPERATION                     OBJECT_NAME
--------------- ----------------------------- ------------
                SELECT STATEMENT
SEL$1             HASH JOIN
SEL$1               TABLE ACCESS FULL           PARENT
SUBQ1               TABLE ACCESS FULL           SUBTEST
SEL$1               TABLE ACCESS FULL           CHILD
```

WILD #16 "NO_PUSH" SQL HINT EXPLAINED

Instead of pushing a subquery earlier, we are going to push it *later*. This example uses the *Scott* schema and a very simple sql. Once again, we will use query block naming to put a label on each clause.

```
Select E.Mgr, D.Loc from Emp E, Dept D
Where E.DeptNo = D.DeptNo
And E.Sal in (Select /*+QB_NAME(CLAUSE1) */
Max(Sal) from Bonus)
And E.Sal in (Select /*+QB_NAME(CLAUSE2) */
Max(HiSal) from Salgrade)
```

The base plan in this test case is interesting, because the subqueries are at the *front*. Oracle has generated the query block name, SEL$1 as the label for the main body of our query.

```
QBLOCK_NAME    OPERATION                          OBJECT_NAME
------------   ---------------------------------  ------------
               SELECT STATEMENT
SEL$1            NESTED LOOPS
                 NESTED LOOPS
SEL$1              TABLE ACCESS FULL               EMP
CLAUSE1            SORT AGGREGATE
CLAUSE1              TABLE ACCESS FULL             BONUS
CLAUSE2            SORT AGGREGATE
CLAUSE2              TABLE ACCESS FULL             SALGRADE
SEL$1              INDEX UNIQUE SCAN               PK_DEPT
SEL$1              TABLE ACCESS BY INDEX ROWID     DEPT
```

Now Do The Push

Now let's see if we can rearrange when the subqueries are considered. Let's try moving processing of *Clause1* to the end of the line, using *No_Push*. (Remember that in Oraclespeak, *No_Push* really means "Push it to the end.") Note the "@" symbol in referencing the subblock:

```
Select /*+NO_PUSH_SUBQ(@CLAUSE1) */
E.Mgr, D.Loc from Emp E, Dept D
Where E.DeptNo = D.DeptNo
And E.Sal in (Select /*+QB_NAME(CLAUSE1) */
Max(Sal) from Bonus)
And E.Sal in (Select /*+QB_NAME(CLAUSE2) */
Max(HiSal) from Salgrade)
```

Once again querying *Plan Table*, we see that the *No_Push_Subq* hint caused Oracle to move *Clause1* to the end:

```
QBLOCK_NAME           OPERATION                      OBJECT_NAME
-----------------     -----------------------        ------------
                      SELECT STATEMENT
SEL$1                   FILTER
                          NESTED LOOPS
                          NESTED LOOPS
SEL$1                       TABLE ACCESS FULL              EMP
CLAUSE2                       SORT AGGREGATE
CLAUSE2                         TABLE ACCESS FULL        SALGRADE
SEL$1                         INDEX UNIQUE SCAN           PK_DEPT
SEL$1                       TABLE ACCESS BY INDEX RO   DEPT
CLAUSE1                   SORT AGGREGATE
CLAUSE1                     TABLE ACCESS FULL             BONUS
```

A Second Push

Similarly, can we move *Clause 2* to the end? We'll just change the hint to this:

```
Select /*+NO_PUSH_SUBQ(@CLAUSE2) */
```

Here is the new plan. We can see that Oracle has moved Clause2 to the end, as expected.

```
QBLOCK_NAME           OPERATION                      OBJECT_NAME
-----------------     -----------------------        ---------------
                      SELECT STATEMENT
SEL$1                   FILTER
                          NESTED LOOPS
                          NESTED LOOPS
SEL$1                       TABLE ACCESS FULL              EMP
CLAUSE1                       SORT AGGREGATE
CLAUSE1                         TABLE ACCESS FULL         BONUS
SEL$1                         INDEX UNIQUE SCAN           PK_DEPT
SEL$1                       TABLE ACCESS BY INDEX ROWID  DEPT
CLAUSE2                   SORT AGGREGATE
CLAUSE2                     TABLE ACCESS FULL             SALGRADE
```